HONG KONG TRAVEL GUIDE 2024

Table of Contents

7. Dining

- Local Cuisine and Food Markets

Conclusion

Embark on an unparalleled journey as you immerse yourself in the heart of this Hong Kong travel guide. Designed not only to provide information but to ignite your imagination, nurture your creativity, and awaken the explorer within, this guide extends an open invitation to step into a realm of discovery that is uniquely your own. Departing from the ordinary, you won't find accompanying images within these pages. Our unwavering belief lies in the notion that the true allure of every encounter is most vividly experienced firsthand, untouched by visual portrayals or preconceived notions.

Visualize each monument, every destination, and even the concealed corners of Hong Kong as exquisite surprises, patiently waiting to amaze and astonish you when you stand in their presence. We are steadfast in our commitment to preserving the thrill of that initial gaze, the sheer wonder that accompanies the revelation of something novel. With this guide as your companion, you stand at the threshold of an extraordinary expedition where curiosity becomes your sole mode of transportation, and this guide becomes your trusted companion. Cast aside any preconceptions and allow yourself to be transported into an authentic Hong Kong of revelations – the magic of your journey commences right here. Remember, though, that the most enchanting images will be those imprinted by your own eyes and cherished within your heart.

In contrast to traditional guidebooks, this volume deliberately omits intricate maps. You might wonder why this intentional omission? Our firm conviction lies in the recognition that the most remarkable discoveries unfurl when you permit yourself to wander, allowing the essence of each place to guide you while embracing the unpredictability of the path. Bid farewell to predefined itineraries and meticulously planned routes, as our aim is to empower you to navigate Hong Kong in your own way, unrestricted by constraints. Embrace the currents of exploration, unveiling hidden treasures that remain undiscovered on conventional maps. Summon the courage to embrace the unfamiliar, trusting your instincts as you boldly venture forth, prepared to be pleasantly surprised – for the enchantment of your journey starts now, in a realm where maps are absent, and the trails reveal themselves with each step. The most extraordinary adventures await within the unexplored folds of the unknown.

Section 1: Introduction to Hong Kong

Hong Kong: A Brief Overview

Nestled on the southeastern coast of China, Hong Kong is a vibrant and dynamic metropolis that effortlessly blends tradition and modernity. A global financial hub, cultural hotspot, and culinary paradise, this Special Administrative Region of China has captivated the world with its unique charm and captivating skyline.

With a history dating back to its days as a British colony, Hong Kong has evolved into a thriving international city that serves as a bridge between the East and the West. Its transformation from a small fishing village to a bustling urban center is a testament to its resilience and adaptability.

One of the most striking features of Hong Kong is its impressive skyline, adorned with towering skyscrapers that seem to reach for the heavens. The city's iconic Victoria Harbour acts as a stunning backdrop, where lights dance on the water's surface during the nightly Symphony of Lights show, a spectacle that showcases the city's artistic prowess.

Beyond the modern façade, Hong Kong's rich cultural heritage continues to thrive. Traditional temples and markets stand in harmony with contemporary galleries and avant-garde installations. The blend of old and new is perhaps most evident in neighborhoods like Central, where gleaming glass towers stand side by side with historical landmarks like Man Mo Temple, enveloping visitors in a sensory journey through time.

Cuisine is an integral part of Hong Kong's identity, and the city boasts a gastronomic scene that is as diverse as its population. From humble street food stalls offering mouthwatering dim sum to high-end restaurants helmed by celebrity chefs, Hong Kong is a paradise for food enthusiasts. The bustling night markets are a must-visit, where the aroma of sizzling delicacies fills the air, tempting locals and visitors alike.

While Hong Kong is synonymous with urban life, its natural beauty is equally captivating. Verdant hiking trails crisscross the mountains that hug the city, offering breathtaking vistas of the skyscrapers below. Beyond the bustling streets, you'll find tranquil beaches where the sound of the waves provides a soothing contrast to the city's energetic pulse.

In addition to its local treasures, Hong Kong serves as a gateway to nearby destinations. A short ferry ride transports travelers to Macau, the "Las Vegas of Asia," with its blend of Portuguese and Chinese influences. Lantau Island beckons with the serene Po Lin Monastery and the towering Tian Tan Buddha, offering a respite from the city's hustle.

Language and culture are integral to understanding Hong Kong's soul. While Cantonese is the primary language spoken, English is widely used, making communication relatively smooth for international visitors. Respect for traditions is deeply ingrained, and visitors are encouraged to observe local customs and etiquette, such as offering and receiving objects with both hands as a sign of respect.

As a global city, Hong Kong is constantly evolving. Its resilience was evident during the protests that dominated headlines, showcasing the passion and determination of its citizens. As the city shapes its future, it remains a beacon of progress, innovation, and adaptability in a rapidly changing world.

In conclusion, Hong Kong is a city of contrasts, where ancient traditions coexist with modern marvels. Its multifaceted personality beckons travelers to explore its bustling streets, savor its culinary delights, and immerse themselves in its cultural tapestry. From towering skyscrapers to tranquil temples, from lively markets to serene beaches, Hong Kong is a destination that promises a sensory journey like no other.

Cultural Diversity: The Heart and Soul of Hong Kong

Nestled at the crossroads of East and West, Hong Kong is a city that thrives on its cultural diversity. With a history marked by colonization, migration, and global trade, this vibrant metropolis has become a melting pot of traditions, languages, and customs that harmoniously coexist, giving rise to a rich tapestry of experiences and identities.

From the moment you step onto the bustling streets of Hong Kong, the fusion of cultures is palpable. The city's origins as a British colony have left an indelible mark on its architecture, legal system, and way of life. Colonial-era buildings stand tall amid modern skyscrapers, a visual testament to the city's complex history.

Hong Kong's cultural diversity is most evident in its people. A true global city, it attracts individuals from all corners of the world, drawn by its economic opportunities and cosmopolitan lifestyle. Expatriates from Europe, North America, and beyond have established vibrant communities, contributing to the city's international flavor.

At the heart of Hong Kong's cultural mosaic is its Chinese heritage. The majority of the population is of Chinese descent, predominantly Cantonese-speaking. Traditional festivals like Chinese New Year and Mid-Autumn Festival are celebrated with fervor, with dragon dances, lantern displays, and sumptuous feasts filling the streets.

Temples and shrines dedicated to various deities dot the cityscape, offering a glimpse into the spiritual practices that have been cherished for generations. Wong Tai Sin Temple, Man Mo Temple, and Po Lin Monastery are among the many sacred sites where visitors can witness the convergence of faith and culture.

Amid the traditional, a vibrant contemporary art scene has taken root. Galleries showcasing the works of local and international artists reflect the city's openness to new ideas and perspectives. Street art adorns hidden alleyways, serving as both a form of self-expression and a commentary on societal issues.

Hong Kong's multiculturalism extends to its palate, with a cuisine that defies categorization. Dim sum, a beloved Cantonese tradition, invites communal dining with an array of savory and sweet dishes. Yet, international flavors also thrive, with Japanese sushi, Indian curries, and Italian pasta sharing the spotlight. The city's night markets and street food stalls are a culinary adventure, where you can savor delicacies from across the globe.

Languages reverberate through the city, reflecting its diverse populace. While Cantonese is the dominant language, English is widely spoken, making it accessible to visitors from English-speaking countries. Additionally, many residents are multilingual, fostering an environment of cross-cultural communication.

Hong Kong's cultural diversity is not without its challenges and complexities. The city has experienced periods of social and political unrest, often rooted in issues of identity and representation. These challenges have sparked important conversations about what it means to be a Hong Konger in a rapidly changing world.

In recent years, the concept of local identity has taken on new dimensions. The younger generation, in particular, is navigating a delicate balance between their Chinese heritage and their distinct Hong Kong identity. This duality is reflected in art, music, and even political movements, shaping the city's future trajectory.

As Hong Kong navigates its place on the global stage, its cultural diversity remains both a strength and a source of resilience. The city's ability to embrace its history while looking forward sets a compelling example for how different cultures can coexist harmoniously, enriching one another in the process.

In conclusion, Hong Kong's cultural diversity is the beating heart of the city. It's a place where centuries-old traditions meld with modern sensibilities, where languages and flavors collide, and where people from all walks of life come together to create a dynamic and ever-evolving urban tapestry. From its neighborhoods to its festivals, from its art to its cuisine, Hong Kong's multicultural essence is a testament to the power of embracing differences and finding unity in diversity.

A Tapestry of Time: The Historical Background of Hong Kong

The history of Hong Kong is a captivating tale that weaves together the threads of colonization, trade, conflict, and resilience. From its humble beginnings as a fishing village to its status as a global financial hub, Hong Kong's journey through time is a testament to the enduring spirit of its people and the forces that shaped its destiny.

Centuries before the iconic skyscrapers adorned the skyline, Hong Kong was a collection of small fishing communities inhabited by the Tanka people. Its strategic location at the mouth of the Pearl River Delta made it a natural trading port, attracting merchants from across the region. This early trade laid the foundation for the cosmopolitan city that Hong Kong would become.

The watershed moment in Hong Kong's history arrived in 1842 with the signing of the Treaty of Nanking, marking the end of the First Opium War between Britain and China. The treaty ceded Hong Kong Island to the British Empire, setting the stage for a new chapter in the city's story. Over the following decades, the British expanded their control to include the Kowloon Peninsula and the New Territories, effectively solidifying their colonial presence.

Under British rule, Hong Kong underwent rapid transformation. The construction of a deepwater harbor and modern infrastructure facilitated global trade, turning the city into a thriving commercial center. Its strategic location made it an ideal gateway to China, and Hong Kong became a hub for merchants, financiers, and entrepreneurs seeking opportunities in the Far East.

As the 20th century unfolded, Hong Kong navigated the challenges posed by world wars, economic fluctuations, and social changes. The Japanese occupation during World War II left scars on the city, but its post-war recovery was swift. The 1950s and 1960s marked a period of industrial growth, with textiles and manufacturing driving the economy. The city's skyline began to take shape, and the construction of public housing aimed to address its burgeoning population.

The latter half of the 20th century witnessed seismic shifts in global geopolitics that would reverberate in Hong Kong. As the British Empire waned, discussions about the city's fate gained momentum. In 1984, the Sino-British Joint Declaration was signed, outlining the "one country, two systems" principle that would govern Hong Kong's transition to Chinese sovereignty in 1997. This arrangement guaranteed the city a high degree of autonomy, preserving its legal and economic systems for 50 years after the handover.

The year 1997 marked a pivotal moment in Hong Kong's history as the Union Jack was lowered and the Chinese flag raised. The handover ceremony symbolized the end of colonial rule and the beginning of a new era under Chinese sovereignty. Anxiety mingled with hope as the city embarked on an unprecedented journey, with its citizens uncertain about the future.

In the years that followed, Hong Kong's resilience was tested by various challenges. Economic crises, outbreaks like the SARS epidemic, and political tensions occasionally cast shadows over the city. Yet, through it all, Hong Kong retained its vibrant spirit. Its people, who had witnessed the city's evolution from British colony to global metropolis, displayed a remarkable ability to adapt and persevere.

The 21st century brought new dynamics into play. The Umbrella Movement in 2014 and the more recent protests in 2019 underscored the deep-seated concerns about political representation and autonomy among Hong Kongers. These events garnered international attention, showcasing the city's determination to safeguard its core values and unique identity.

As Hong Kong continues to evolve, its historical legacy remains embedded in its urban fabric. Colonial-era buildings stand as witnesses to a bygone era, while modern architecture testifies to the city's rapid growth and cosmopolitan aspirations. Museums and heritage sites provide glimpses into the stories of its past, preserving the memories of those who shaped its trajectory.

In conclusion, Hong Kong's historical background is a tale of transformation, resilience, and cultural convergence. From its origins as a trading port to its present status as a global financial powerhouse, the city's journey has been marked by challenges, triumphs, and the indomitable spirit of its people. The threads of history are interwoven with the fabric of its streets, the diversity of its neighborhoods, and the aspirations of its citizens, creating a tapestry that tells a story of the past, present, and the possibilities of the future.

Section 2: Planning Your Trip

The Perfect Moment: Deciding the Best Time to Visit Hong Kong

Hong Kong, a dynamic city of towering skyscrapers, bustling markets, and vibrant neighborhoods, beckons travelers year-round with its captivating blend of East-meets-West culture and stunning cityscapes. While this bustling metropolis is a year-round destination, the best time to visit often depends on individual preferences, interests, and weather considerations. From the vibrant festivities of festivals to the more temperate months, Hong Kong offers diverse experiences that cater to a variety of tastes.

Spring (March to May): Blooms and Pleasant Weather

Spring emerges as a favorable time to explore Hong Kong, with the weather transitioning from the cool winter months to a more pleasant and mild atmosphere. Temperatures range between 18°C and 24°C (64°F to 75°F), making it a comfortable time for outdoor activities and sightseeing. This period is also marked by the colorful blooms of cherry blossoms and other flowers, adding a touch of natural beauty to the city's urban landscape. The Hong Kong Arts Festival, showcasing an array of artistic performances, further enhances the cultural scene during this season.

Summer (June to August): Vibrant Festivities and Warmth

The summer months in Hong Kong are characterized by warm and humid weather, with temperatures averaging around 28°C to 31°C (82°F to 88°F). Despite the heat, summer holds its own allure, particularly for those who enjoy vibrant festivals and beachside relaxation. The Dragon Boat Festival, with its thrilling boat races and traditional rice dumplings, adds a cultural touch to the season. Beachgoers can bask in the sun and enjoy the city's numerous beaches, including Repulse Bay and Shek O Beach.

Autumn (September to November): Mild Weather and Outdoor Exploration

Autumn emerges as a favorite time for many travelers due to its pleasant climate, lower humidity, and fewer crowds. Temperatures hover around 22°C to 28°C (72°F to 82°F), providing comfortable conditions for outdoor exploration and sightseeing. The Mid-Autumn Festival, celebrated with vibrant lantern displays and mooncakes, adds a touch of enchantment to the city's ambiance. Autumn is also a prime time for hiking, as the slightly cooler weather enhances the experience on the city's picturesque trails.

Winter (December to February): Mild Temperatures and Cultural Experiences

Winter in Hong Kong is mild, with temperatures ranging from 15°C to 20°C (59°F to 68°F). While not as cold as many other destinations during this time, it offers a pleasant escape for those seeking a cooler climate. The WinterFest, featuring ice skating rinks and festive decorations, brings a touch of holiday spirit to the city. Additionally, the Chinese New Year celebrations, characterized by lively parades, traditional performances, and vibrant decorations, provide a cultural immersion into Hong Kong's heritage.

Considerations for Timing Your Visit

When deciding the best time to visit Hong Kong, several factors come into play:

- Weather: Hong Kong's subtropical climate influences the choice of clothing and outdoor activities. While mild temperatures can be enjoyed year-round, visitors may prefer the more temperate weather of spring and autumn for comfortable exploration.

- Crowds: High tourist seasons often bring larger crowds to popular attractions. Those seeking a quieter experience might consider visiting during the shoulder seasons of spring and autumn.

- Festivals and Events: Hong Kong's festive calendar is brimming with cultural events and celebrations. Those interested in experiencing local traditions and vibrant festivals should time their visit accordingly.

- Budget: Travel costs can fluctuate based on high and low seasons. While travel deals might be more readily available during the off-peak months, it's important to weigh this against factors like weather and festival opportunities.

-

In conclusion, choosing the best time to visit Hong Kong ultimately depends on personal preferences and what you aim to experience during your trip. Whether you're captivated by the vibrancy of summer festivals, the cultural charm of autumn celebrations, or the mild weather of spring and winter, Hong Kong offers a diverse array of experiences year-round. From dynamic street markets to tranquil parks, from traditional temples to contemporary art galleries, this bustling city promises a memorable adventure whenever you choose to embark on it.

Navigating Borders: Visa and Entry Requirements for Hong Kong Travel

Hong Kong, with its iconic skyline, vibrant culture, and global connections, attracts visitors from around the world. As you prepare to embark on your journey to this dynamic city, understanding the visa and entry requirements is essential to ensure a smooth and hassle-free travel experience. Whether you're planning a short vacation or a more extended stay, here's a comprehensive overview of the visa and entry regulations for Hong Kong.

Visa-Free Access: Welcoming Many Nationalities

One of the advantages of visiting Hong Kong is its lenient visa policy, which grants visa-free access to nationals of many countries for short stays. Generally, visitors from countries like the United States, Canada, the United Kingdom, Australia, and many European nations can enter Hong Kong without a visa and stay for a certain period, usually ranging from 7 to 180 days, depending on their nationality. It's important to note that the specific duration of stay and other conditions can vary based on your passport's country of issuance.

Visa-On-Arrival: Flexibility for Certain Nationalities

For some nationalities that aren't eligible for visa-free access, Hong Kong offers a visa-on-arrival option. This allows travelers to obtain their visa upon landing at the airport, granting them entry for a specified duration. This flexibility can be particularly beneficial for last-minute trips or travelers who haven't had the opportunity to apply for a visa in advance.

Pre-Arrival Visa Application: Longer Stays and Specific Purposes

While many visitors can enter Hong Kong without a visa for short stays, there are situations where obtaining a pre-arrival visa is necessary or advisable. If you plan to stay for an extended period, pursue studies, work, or engage in certain business activities, you'll likely need to apply for a visa in advance.

The Hong Kong Immigration Department offers various visa categories to accommodate different purposes, such as employment, investment, study, and training. These visas require applicants to provide relevant documentation, including sponsorship letters, proof of financial stability, and educational qualifications, depending on the nature of the visit. It's essential to review the specific requirements for your intended purpose to ensure a successful application process.

Mainland China and Special Administrative Region (SAR) Visas: Unique Considerations

While Hong Kong is a Special Administrative Region (SAR) of China, it maintains separate immigration policies from mainland China. This means that if you plan to travel between mainland China and Hong Kong, you might need to obtain different visas for each destination, even if you're using the same passport.

Travelers often have the opportunity to use the Individual Visit Scheme (IVS), which allows residents of certain mainland Chinese cities to visit Hong Kong on a more flexible basis. This scheme has played a significant role in promoting cross-border tourism and business interactions.

Practical Application: Ensuring a Smooth Journey

Before embarking on your trip to Hong Kong, there are several key steps to follow to ensure a seamless entry process:

1. Check Visa Requirements: Start by checking whether your nationality requires a visa for Hong Kong and what the specific conditions are for your visit.

2. Application Process: If you need a pre-arrival visa for a longer stay or specific purpose, gather all required documentation and submit your application well in advance. This will help avoid any last-minute complications.

3. Duration of Stay: Understand the maximum length of stay allowed under your visa type. Overstaying your visa can result in fines, deportation, or even a ban from re-entering Hong Kong.

4. Entry Port: Make sure to arrive at a recognized entry port, such as Hong Kong International Airport or specific border crossings, to facilitate a smooth entry process.

5. Travel Insurance: It's advisable to have travel insurance that covers unexpected events, including medical emergencies and trip cancellations, to ensure you're protected during your journey.

In conclusion, Hong Kong's visa and entry requirements cater to a wide range of travelers, from short-term tourists to those seeking more extended stays for various purposes. The city's accessible policies make it a welcoming destination for visitors from around the globe. To ensure a successful and enjoyable trip, it's essential to familiarize yourself with the specific visa regulations that apply to your situation and to plan ahead by gathering the necessary documentation, understanding the conditions of your visit, and complying with immigration guidelines. With the right preparations, you can look forward to a memorable experience exploring the captivating landscapes, cultural treasures, and urban wonders of Hong Kong.

Navigating the Monetary Maze: Currency and Money Matters in Hong Kong

When venturing into the vibrant streets of Hong Kong, you'll find yourself immersed in a world of stunning architecture, delectable cuisine, and bustling markets. As you embark on this journey, it's crucial to understand the currency and money matters that will shape your experience. From the local currency to banking options and spending considerations, here's a comprehensive overview of how to navigate the financial landscape during your time in this dynamic city.

The Hong Kong Dollar (HKD): Your Currency Companion

The official currency of Hong Kong is the Hong Kong Dollar (HKD). This vibrant currency comes in various denominations, from coins to banknotes, each adorned with iconic images representing the city's rich history and culture. The HKD is abbreviated as "$" and is often symbolized by the sign "HK$."

The Hong Kong Dollar is further divided into subunits, with one dollar consisting of 100 cents. Coins are commonly found in denominations of 10 cents, 20 cents, 50 cents, 1 dollar, 2 dollars, and 5 dollars. Banknotes are issued in values of 10 dollars, 20 dollars, 50 dollars, 100 dollars, 500 dollars, and 1,000 dollars. Familiarizing yourself with these denominations will help you manage your transactions and expenditures effectively.

Currency Exchange: Where and How

Arriving in Hong Kong with foreign currency? You'll find numerous options for exchanging your money into Hong Kong Dollars. Currency exchange services are available at the Hong Kong International Airport, banks, money changers, and currency exchange kiosks located throughout the city. While exchange rates may vary slightly between different providers, it's wise to compare rates and fees to secure the best deal.

Banks are a reliable choice for currency exchange, often offering competitive rates and a straightforward process. Keep in mind that many banks have specific operating hours, so it's advisable to plan your currency exchange during regular business hours.

Plastic Power: Credit and Debit Cards

Credit and debit cards are widely accepted in Hong Kong, making them a convenient and secure method of payment. Major international cards such as Visa, MasterCard, American Express, and UnionPay are recognized at hotels, restaurants, retail stores, and even public transportation systems.

ATMs (Automated Teller Machines) are abundant across the city and allow you to withdraw Hong Kong Dollars directly from your bank account back home. Be sure to check with your bank about any associated fees for international transactions or currency conversion. Using a debit card for ATM withdrawals can often provide you with competitive exchange rates.

Cash vs. Cards: Finding the Balance

While electronic payment methods are prevalent, carrying a reasonable amount of local currency is still recommended, especially when visiting smaller establishments, street markets, or places that may not accept cards. Cash is handy for tipping, local transportation, and making purchases in traditional markets or small shops.

Remember that currency exchange rates can vary, so it's essential to stay informed and check rates regularly to make the most of your money. Utilize currency conversion apps or websites to estimate costs accurately and ensure that you're getting the best value for your currency.

Tipping Etiquette: A Cultural Consideration

Tipping practices in Hong Kong are influenced by both Western customs and local norms. Tipping is not mandatory but is appreciated for good service. In restaurants, a 10% service charge is often included in the bill. If it's not included, leaving a 10-15% tip is customary. For other services, like hotel staff and tour guides, a small gratuity is a thoughtful gesture.

Budgeting and Cost Considerations

Hong Kong offers a wide range of experiences to suit various budgets. While the city can be perceived as expensive due to its high-end shopping and dining options, there are also plenty of affordable choices, including street food stalls, local markets, and budget accommodations.

To manage your expenses effectively, it's advisable to set a daily budget that includes accommodation, food, transportation, and entertainment. Researching prices beforehand and

considering any planned activities or shopping can help you establish a realistic budget that aligns with your travel goals.

In conclusion, understanding the currency and money matters in Hong Kong is essential for a seamless and enjoyable travel experience. The Hong Kong Dollar is the gateway to exploring this vibrant city, and knowing where and how to exchange your currency can save you time and money. Credit and debit cards offer convenience and security, but carrying cash for smaller transactions is also recommended. By being mindful of tipping etiquette and budget considerations, you'll be well-prepared to embark on a financial journey that complements your exploration of Hong Kong's dynamic landscapes, cultural treasures, and urban wonders.

Preserving Well-being: Health and Safety Tips for a Journey to Hong Kong

Embarking on a journey to the vibrant city of Hong Kong promises an array of unforgettable experiences, from exploring bustling markets to savoring delectable cuisine and admiring iconic skyline views. Amid the excitement of travel, prioritizing your health and safety is paramount to ensure a smooth and enjoyable adventure. By staying informed about local health precautions, understanding safety measures, and practicing responsible travel habits, you can fully embrace the wonders of Hong Kong while safeguarding your well-being.

Health Precautions: Staying Informed and Prepared

Before traveling to Hong Kong, it's essential to be aware of any health precautions, vaccinations, or health advisories that may apply to your trip. While Hong Kong is generally considered safe for travelers, certain health considerations can enhance your travel experience:

1. Vaccinations: Check with your healthcare provider to ensure that your routine vaccinations are up to date. Depending on your travel plans and medical history, you may also need additional vaccinations, such as hepatitis A and B, typhoid, or influenza.

2. Medical Insurance: Prior to departure, confirm that your travel insurance covers medical emergencies and healthcare expenses abroad. Having comprehensive coverage can provide peace of mind in case unexpected health issues arise during your trip.

3. Medications: If you take prescription medications, ensure that you have an adequate supply for the duration of your trip. It's also wise to carry a copy of your prescriptions and a note from your doctor explaining the medical necessity of your medications.

4. Water and Food Safety: Tap water in Hong Kong is generally safe to drink, but some travelers prefer bottled water. When dining, opt for well-established restaurants and eateries to reduce the risk of foodborne illnesses. Street food is popular and delicious, but consider consuming items that are cooked fresh in front of you.

Safety Measures: Navigating Urban Landscapes

Hong Kong is a safe destination for travelers, boasting low crime rates and a well-developed infrastructure. However, it's essential to stay vigilant and follow common safety guidelines:

1. Personal Belongings: Like any major city, Hong Kong experiences occasional incidents of petty theft. Keep an eye on your belongings, especially in crowded places like markets and public transportation. Use a money belt or secure pouch to safeguard important documents and valuables.

2. Transportation Safety: Hong Kong's public transportation system is efficient and safe. When using the MTR (Mass Transit Railway) or buses, be mindful of your belongings, especially during

peak hours. Taxis are also a reliable mode of transport, but choose licensed taxis and ask the driver to use the meter.

3. Emergency Numbers: Familiarize yourself with local emergency numbers, including the police (999) and medical services (999 or 120), should you require assistance.

Responsible Travel: Ethical Considerations

Responsible travel involves more than just personal safety; it extends to preserving the environment, respecting local culture, and contributing positively to the communities you visit:

1. Environmental Respect: Hong Kong's natural landscapes are a treasure. Follow Leave No Trace principles by not littering, staying on designated paths, and refraining from disturbing wildlife.

2. Cultural Sensitivity: Hong Kong is a culturally diverse city, and it's essential to respect local customs and traditions. When visiting temples and other religious sites, dress modestly and behave respectfully. Ask for permission before taking photographs of people.

3. Public Spaces: Keep in mind that smoking is prohibited in most indoor public spaces, including restaurants, shopping malls, and public transportation. Adhering to local regulations helps maintain a healthy environment for all.

4. Environmental Conservation: The ocean and marine life play a significant role in Hong Kong's ecosystem. When engaging in water-based activities, such as snorkeling or diving, ensure that you choose operators committed to responsible tourism practices that minimize the impact on aquatic environments.

Preparedness and Mindfulness: Your Travel Allies

While embarking on your adventure to Hong Kong, being prepared and practicing mindfulness are your greatest allies for health and safety:

- Stay Informed: Stay updated about any travel advisories, health alerts, or local news that may affect your trip.

- Stay Connected: Share your itinerary and contact information with a friend or family member back home. Having a means of communication can be invaluable in case of emergencies.

- Stay Open-minded: Immerse yourself in local experiences, but trust your instincts and exercise caution when trying new activities or interacting with unfamiliar individuals.

- Stay Hydrated and Rested: The excitement of travel can sometimes lead to neglecting your basic needs. Stay hydrated, get enough rest, and listen to your body.

In conclusion, embarking on a journey to Hong Kong presents an opportunity to create lifelong memories and explore a vibrant cultural landscape. By prioritizing your health and safety through proactive measures, informed decisions, and responsible travel practices, you can fully enjoy the dynamic urban wonders, culinary delights, and breathtaking landscapes that Hong Kong has to offer. By striking a balance between adventure and well-being, you'll embark on a journey that combines exploration with the peace of mind that comes from knowing you've taken the necessary steps to ensure your health and safety are a top priority.

The Essential Packing Guide for Your Hong Kong Adventure

Embarking on a journey to Hong Kong, a captivating blend of culture, modernity, and natural beauty, requires careful preparation when it comes to packing. A well-curated suitcase ensures that you have everything you need for a seamless and enjoyable adventure. Whether you're a seasoned traveler or venturing out for the first time, this comprehensive packing guide will help you prepare for the diverse experiences that await you in this vibrant city.

Clothing Essentials: Dressing for Hong Kong's Climate

Hong Kong's climate is characterized by its subtropical nature, with distinct seasons that influence your packing choices:

- Light and Breathable Clothing: Pack lightweight and breathable clothing suitable for warm and humid weather. Cotton fabrics and moisture-wicking materials are ideal to keep you comfortable while exploring the city.

- Rain Gear: While Hong Kong enjoys plenty of sunshine, sudden rain showers are common, especially during the summer months. A compact and portable umbrella or a lightweight rain jacket can come in handy.

- Layers: For the cooler months, especially autumn and winter, consider layering your clothing. A light sweater or jacket can provide warmth during breezy evenings.

- Comfortable Shoes: Comfortable walking shoes are a must. You'll likely be exploring on foot, so choose footwear that provides support and is suitable for walking on different surfaces.

Travel Essentials: Practical Items for Your Adventure

As you prepare to embark on your Hong Kong adventure, consider including these practical items in your suitcase:

- Travel Adapters: Hong Kong uses a Type G electrical outlet. Don't forget to pack travel adapters to ensure you can charge your devices without any issues.

- Portable Charger: Keep your devices charged and ready for capturing memories by including a portable charger in your bag.

- Reusable Water Bottle: Staying hydrated is crucial. A reusable water bottle with a filter can help you stay refreshed without relying on single-use plastic bottles.

- Daypack or Tote Bag: A compact daypack or tote bag is handy for carrying essentials like a water bottle, sunscreen, and a map while exploring the city.

Electronics and Gadgets: Staying Connected

To capture the moments, stay connected, and navigate the city efficiently, consider these electronic essentials:

- Smartphone: Your smartphone is a versatile tool for maps, communication, and photography.

- Camera: If you're a photography enthusiast, don't forget to bring your camera to capture the stunning cityscapes and landscapes.

- Power Bank: Keep your devices charged on the go with a reliable power bank.

Documents and Essentials: Navigating Seamlessly

To ensure a smooth journey and hassle-free entry, organize your documents and essential items:

- Passport and Visa: Ensure your passport is valid for the duration of your trip, and carry any required visas or entry documents.

- Travel Insurance: Have a printed copy of your travel insurance policy and contact information in case of emergencies.

- Prescriptions and Medications: Carry prescription medications in their original packaging along with a copy of your prescription from your doctor.

- Local Currency: While credit and debit cards are widely accepted, having a small amount of local currency on hand is useful for small purchases and tips.

Personal Care and Health: Staying Comfortable and Healthy

Pack personal care items to ensure your comfort and well-being during your trip:

- Sun Protection: Hong Kong's sunny climate calls for sun protection. Pack sunscreen, sunglasses, and a wide-brimmed hat to shield yourself from the sun.

- Insect Repellent: Depending on the season and your activities, insect repellent can be useful to ward off mosquitoes.

- Basic First Aid Kit: Include essentials like adhesive bandages, pain relievers, and any personal medications you may need.

Optional Items: Tailoring Your Experience

Depending on your interests and activities, consider these optional items to enhance your experience:

- Guidebook or Maps: Having a guidebook or maps can be helpful for navigating the city and discovering hidden gems.

- Reusable Shopping Bag: Hong Kong is a shopper's paradise. A reusable shopping bag can be handy for carrying your purchases.

- Swimsuit and Beach Gear: If you plan to visit the city's beautiful beaches, pack your swimsuit and beach essentials.

- Language Guide or App: While English is widely spoken, a basic language guide or translation app can be useful for communication.

Remember: Less Is More

While it's tempting to pack for every possible scenario, remember that Hong Kong offers a range of shopping options if you find you've forgotten something. Packing efficiently and prioritizing essential items will help keep your suitcase light and manageable.

In conclusion, preparing for your Hong Kong adventure involves a balance of practicality, comfort, and preparation for various experiences. By packing clothing suitable for the climate, essential travel items, electronics, documents, personal care essentials, and optional items tailored to your interests, you'll be well-equipped to embrace the city's dynamic culture, breathtaking landscapes, and urban marvels. A well-curated suitcase ensures that you can navigate the city with ease, capturing moments, staying comfortable, and enjoying all that Hong Kong has to offer.

Section 3: Getting to Hong Kong

I.   Flights and Airports

Hong Kong, a global hub known for its modernity and connectivity, boasts world-class airports and a wide range of flight options. If you're planning a trip to this vibrant city, understanding the best flights and airports will be instrumental in ensuring a smooth and convenient travel experience. Here's a guide to help you navigate the options for reaching and departing from Hong Kong.

Airports in Hong Kong: The Gateways to the City

Hong Kong is served by two major airports that cater to both international and regional flights:

1. Hong Kong International Airport (HKG): Also known as Chek Lap Kok Airport, HKG is one of the world's busiest and most modern airports. Located on Chek Lap Kok Island, this state-of-the-art facility is known for its efficiency, connectivity, and world-class amenities. It features two terminals, Terminal 1 and Terminal 2, connected by the automated SkyPlaza shopping and entertainment complex. HKG offers a wide range of

dining options, duty-free shopping, lounges, and convenient transportation connections to the city center.

2. Shenzhen Bao'an International Airport (SZX): While technically not in Hong Kong, Shenzhen Bao'an International Airport serves as an alternative option for travelers visiting Hong Kong. Located in Shenzhen, mainland China, just across the border from Hong Kong, SZX is well-connected to the city via various transportation options. It's a convenient choice for travelers who want to explore both Shenzhen and Hong Kong during their trip.

Finding the Best Flights: Considerations

When searching for the best flights to Hong Kong, consider the following factors to tailor your choice to your preferences and needs:

- Flight Routes: Hong Kong's international airport is well-connected to major cities around the world, making it relatively easy to find direct flights or convenient layovers.

- Airlines: A variety of airlines operate flights to and from Hong Kong, ranging from full-service carriers to budget airlines. Consider your preferred airline, cabin class, and service options.

- Travel Dates: Flights to Hong Kong may vary in price depending on the time of year, holidays, and events. Being flexible with your travel dates can help you secure better deals.

- Direct vs. Connecting Flights: Depending on your departure location and budget, you can choose between direct flights or those with layovers. Direct flights are often more convenient, but connecting flights may offer better pricing.

- Flight Duration: Flight durations can vary based on the departure location and layovers. Consider your comfort level with longer flights versus shorter travel times.

Booking Your Flights: Tips for Smart Choices

To ensure you're making smart choices when booking your flights to and from Hong Kong, keep these tips in mind:

- Compare Prices: Utilize flight comparison websites to compare prices and options across various airlines. This will help you find the best deals.

- Book in Advance: Booking your flights well in advance can often lead to better prices and availability, especially during peak travel seasons.

- Flexible Dates: If your travel dates are flexible, use fare comparison tools that show you the prices across a range of dates. This can help you identify the most affordable options.

- Frequent Flyer Programs: If you're a member of a frequent flyer program, consider using your miles to book flights or earn additional rewards.

Transportation Between Airports and the City

Both Hong Kong International Airport (HKG) and Shenzhen Bao'an International Airport (SZX) offer efficient transportation options to the city center:

- HKG: The Airport Express is a dedicated train service that connects HKG to various locations in Hong Kong, including Hong Kong Station, Kowloon Station, and Tsing Yi Station. Taxis, buses, and private transfer services are also available.

- SZX: From Shenzhen Bao'an International Airport, you can take the Airport Shuttle Bus to the border checkpoint and then proceed to Hong Kong via train or taxi. The Huanggang Port is a popular crossing point for travelers going between Shenzhen and Hong Kong.

In conclusion, Hong Kong's two major airports, Hong Kong International Airport (HKG) and Shenzhen Bao'an International Airport (SZX), offer convenient gateways for travelers from around the world. When searching for the best flights, consider factors like flight routes, airlines, travel dates, and connectivity. Booking in advance and comparing prices across platforms can help you secure the most favorable deals. Once you've landed, efficient transportation options ensure that you can quickly reach the heart of Hong Kong and begin your exploration of this captivating city.

A. Hong Kong International Airport (HKG): A Gateway to Excellence

Nestled on the island of Chek Lap Kok, Hong Kong International Airport (HKG) stands as a testament to modern engineering, efficiency, and innovation. Renowned for its state-of-the-art facilities, connectivity, and impressive design, HKG has earned its reputation as one of the world's premier airports. Serving as a gateway to both Hong Kong and the world, this bustling hub offers travelers a seamless and memorable experience from the moment they arrive to the moment they depart.

The story of Hong Kong International Airport began with a vision to create a world-class aviation hub capable of accommodating the city's growing demand for air travel. Prior to its construction, the old Kai Tak Airport had outgrown its capacity and was known for its challenging and dramatic approach that took planes over the heart of the city. Thus, the ambitious Chek Lap Kok project was born, aiming to create a modern airport that would redefine the travel experience.

HKG's design is a marvel of engineering and efficiency. Spread over approximately 1,255 hectares of reclaimed land, the airport boasts two passenger terminals, aptly named Terminal 1 and Terminal 2. These terminals are connected by the SkyPlaza, a shopping and entertainment complex that provides travelers with a variety of dining, shopping, and leisure options.

Terminal 1, the larger of the two, is an architectural masterpiece characterized by its sweeping curves and expansive spaces. Its efficient layout ensures smooth passenger flow, while its glass façade allows ample natural light to flood the interior. Terminal 2 caters to budget airlines and offers a more compact yet equally functional space.

HKG is a global aviation hub that connects Hong Kong with countless cities across the world. The airport serves as a base for a multitude of airlines, making it a focal point for both regional and international travel. With its strategic location in the heart of Asia, HKG is a popular stopover for long-haul flights and offers an array of connecting options.

Passengers passing through HKG are treated to a world of services and amenities that cater to every need. From lounges and duty-free shopping to premium services like fast-track immigration, the airport prides itself on providing a comprehensive and pleasant experience for travelers.

Efficiency is at the core of HKG's design, and this extends beyond the terminals to the transportation options available to and from the airport. The Airport Express, a dedicated train service, seamlessly connects the airport with key destinations in Hong Kong. Passengers can

travel comfortably and swiftly to Hong Kong Station, Kowloon Station, and Tsing Yi Station. This convenience makes the transition from air to land a breeze, allowing travelers to reach their destinations with ease.

HKG is not only a pioneer in modern air travel but also a leader in sustainability and environmental stewardship. The airport is committed to reducing its carbon footprint and enhancing its green initiatives. Solar panels, energy-efficient lighting, and waste reduction measures are among the sustainable practices that contribute to its status as an environmentally conscious aviation hub.

The SkyPlaza within HKG is a world of shopping and dining, offering an array of international brands, boutiques, and eateries. Travelers can indulge in retail therapy, sample international cuisines, or simply relax with a cup of coffee while awaiting their flights. The vibrant atmosphere and diverse offerings make SkyPlaza a destination in itself.

Hong Kong International Airport isn't just a transit hub; it's also a cultural contributor. The airport frequently hosts events, exhibitions, and installations that celebrate Hong Kong's artistic and cultural heritage. From interactive displays to art installations, HKG offers passengers a taste of the city's vibrant creativity.

Whether travelers are arriving in Hong Kong or bidding the city farewell, Hong Kong International Airport leaves a lasting impression. From its sleek design and efficient layout to its global connectivity and commitment to sustainability, HKG embodies the spirit of modern travel. As passengers pass through its terminals, they are greeted by a glimpse of Hong Kong's dynamism and efficiency, setting the tone for the adventures that await them in the city and beyond.

A Vision Realized: The Inception of Hong Kong International Airport (HKG)

In the annals of modern aviation history, Hong Kong International Airport (HKG) stands as a remarkable testament to human ingenuity, perseverance, and the realization of a visionary dream. This sprawling aviation marvel, situated on the reclaimed land of Chek Lap Kok Island, serves as a gateway to the bustling metropolis of Hong Kong and embodies a story of ambition, innovation, and the pursuit of excellence.

The journey to the creation of HKG was prompted by a pressing need for a modern and efficient aviation hub to replace Hong Kong's former airport, Kai Tak. Kai Tak, situated in the heart of

Kowloon, had gained notoriety for its precarious approach over the city's densely populated areas. As air travel continued to expand and evolve, the limitations of Kai Tak became increasingly evident. The city required an airport that could not only accommodate the growing number of passengers but also provide a safer and more efficient experience for both travelers and aviation professionals.

The realization of this vision led to the ambitious Chek Lap Kok project—a massive undertaking that involved the reclamation of land from the sea to build a new airport facility. Named after the island upon which it was situated, the Chek Lap Kok project was marked by its audacity and scale. The objective was clear: to construct an airport that could serve as a world-class aviation hub, capable of meeting the demands of a rapidly changing travel landscape.

The construction of HKG was a feat of modern engineering that spanned years of planning, innovation, and construction. Envisioned as more than just an airport, HKG was designed to be a dynamic and efficient facility that could seamlessly handle the influx of passengers, cargo, and aircraft from around the globe.

The reclamation process itself was a groundbreaking endeavor, involving the creation of a vast platform of land from the sea. Enormous quantities of rock and soil were reclaimed, reshaped, and fortified to create a foundation that could support the weight and activity of a bustling airport.

One of the hallmarks of HKG's design is its emphasis on efficiency and passenger convenience. The airport features two main passenger terminals: Terminal 1 and Terminal 2. Terminal 1, with its iconic curved roof and expansive spaces, serves as the main international gateway. Its design focuses on providing seamless passenger flow, ample natural light, and a welcoming atmosphere. Terminal 2, designed to accommodate budget airlines, offers a more compact yet functional space that maintains the same commitment to efficiency.

The completion of HKG marked the emergence of a truly global aviation hub, strategically positioned in the heart of Asia. With its extensive network of flights connecting Hong Kong to major cities around the world, the airport became a crossroads for international travel. Travelers from diverse backgrounds and cultures converge at HKG, transforming the airport into a microcosm of the world's bustling movement.

The realization of HKG was not merely a construction project; it was the birth of an aviation legacy. The airport's design, engineering, and operational efficiency set new benchmarks for what an aviation hub could achieve. Its establishment was a testament to the vision of progress and the commitment to creating a facility that would not only serve the city's immediate needs but also shape the future of air travel.

As travelers arrive at HKG, they are greeted not only by its stunning architecture and state-of-the-art facilities but also by the embodiment of a dream that became a reality. This airport

represents the convergence of innovation, ambition, and the relentless pursuit of excellence—a reminder that the sky is not the limit when it comes to human potential.

In conclusion, the inception of Hong Kong International Airport is a story that encapsulates the spirit of human endeavor. From the need for progress to the realization of an audacious vision, HKG's journey from concept to reality reflects the heights that can be reached when innovation, determination, and purpose converge. As travelers traverse its terminals, they step into a legacy that celebrates the power of human ingenuity and leaves an indelible mark on the history of aviation.

Efficient Design and Innovation: The Heartbeat of Hong Kong International Airport

Nestled on the reclaimed land of Chek Lap Kok Island, Hong Kong International Airport (HKG) stands as a testament to efficient design and relentless innovation. This bustling aviation hub showcases an architecture that not only captivates the eye but also streamlines the travel experience for millions of passengers each year. From its iconic terminals to state-of-the-art facilities, HKG's commitment to efficiency and innovation reverberates throughout every corner of this modern marvel.

Terminal 1, the larger of the two passenger terminals at HKG, is a symphony of architecture, function, and aesthetics. Designed to embody the principles of efficiency and passenger convenience, it stands as a testament to what an airport terminal can achieve. The curvilinear roof, a hallmark of Terminal 1's design, not only adds a visually stunning element but also serves a practical purpose by maximizing natural light and minimizing the need for excessive artificial lighting during the day.

Inside Terminal 1, a spacious and intuitive layout ensures a seamless flow of passengers. The vast check-in hall is equipped with multiple counters, reducing wait times and accommodating the constant influx of travelers. The efficient baggage handling system ensures that luggage moves swiftly from check-in to departure gates, enhancing both passenger experience and operational efficiency.

HKG's innovation extends beyond its architectural design. The airport continuously seeks new ways to enhance the passenger experience through technology and modern amenities. Interactive information kiosks provide real-time flight updates, wayfinding assistance, and information about airport services. Digital displays throughout the terminal guide passengers to their gates and offer insights into retail and dining options.

Automated self-check-in kiosks streamline the check-in process, allowing passengers to print boarding passes and baggage tags on their own, reducing queues and wait times. The adoption of biometric technology for immigration and security clearance further expedites the passage of travelers through the airport.

HKG's dedication to innovation is evident in its SkyPlaza—an integrated shopping and entertainment complex that serves as a dynamic extension of the airport experience. SkyPlaza offers a multitude of dining, shopping, and leisure options, creating an environment that encourages passengers to explore, relax, and engage.

The aviation-themed Dream Come True Education Park within SkyPlaza provides an educational and interactive experience for children, immersing them in the world of aviation and inspiring the next generation of travelers and aviation enthusiasts.

HKG's commitment to innovation aligns harmoniously with its dedication to sustainability. The airport has incorporated environmentally friendly practices into its operations and infrastructure. The South Runway, for instance, utilizes an innovative reclamation method that reduces the amount of concrete required, minimizing environmental impact. Furthermore, the installation of solar panels, energy-efficient lighting systems, and waste reduction initiatives showcases HKG's focus on long-term sustainability.

Terminal 2, another testament to efficiency, caters to the needs of budget airlines and their passengers. While smaller in scale compared to Terminal 1, Terminal 2's layout and design principles remain consistent, focusing on passenger flow, ease of navigation, and convenience.

As technology evolves and the demands of travel change, HKG continues to innovate to stay ahead of the curve. The airport invests in research and development to explore cutting-edge solutions that can further enhance operational efficiency, passenger experience, and sustainability.

The efficient design and innovation embodied by HKG have created a legacy that reverberates across the aviation industry. Beyond its striking architecture, the airport's efficiency enhances the travel experience, reduces operational costs, and contributes to the overall success of the facility. With a constant eye on the future, HKG remains dedicated to pushing the boundaries of what an airport can achieve, while keeping passenger needs and global sustainability in mind.

In conclusion, Hong Kong International Airport's efficient design and innovation intertwine to create an aviation hub that is both visually captivating and functionally exceptional. The marriage of aesthetics and practicality, the integration of technology, and the commitment to sustainability showcase an airport that is more than just a transit point—it is an embodiment of progress and human creativity. As HKG continues to adapt and evolve, it sets a remarkable precedent for the airports of tomorrow, inspiring travelers and the industry at large to embrace the endless possibilities of efficient design and innovation.

Global Connectivity: Hong Kong International Airport's Role as a Hub of International Travel

In the heart of the bustling metropolis of Hong Kong lies an aviation marvel that serves as a global crossroads—Hong Kong International Airport (HKG). With its strategic location, world-class facilities, and extensive network of flights, HKG stands as a beacon of global connectivity, facilitating the movement of travelers, cultures, and commerce across the world. As one of the world's busiest and most efficient airports, HKG plays a pivotal role in shaping the landscape of international travel.

HKG's significance as a hub of international travel is deeply rooted in its geographical positioning. Situated in close proximity to major cities in Asia and the Pacific, the airport serves as a natural gateway to the continent. This strategic location not only makes HKG a convenient stopover for travelers connecting between different regions but also positions the airport as an ideal entry point for those exploring Asia and beyond.

One of HKG's most defining features is its extensive network of flights that connect the airport to cities across the globe. From North America to Europe, Africa to Oceania, the airport serves as a launchpad for countless journeys. Major international airlines, as well as regional carriers, operate routes to and from HKG, making it a diverse and bustling hub that caters to a wide range of travel preferences and itineraries.

As travelers converge at HKG from every corner of the world, the airport becomes a microcosm of global cultures, languages, and traditions. The diverse array of nationalities and backgrounds creates an atmosphere that celebrates the unity of human exploration while honoring the rich tapestry of diversity. In a matter of hours, passengers can transition from one cultural sphere to another, experiencing the richness of global heritage in a singular setting.

Beyond facilitating the movement of passengers, HKG also plays a critical role in global trade and commerce. With its efficient cargo facilities and strategic connections, the airport serves as a hub for transporting goods and merchandise between different continents. High-value cargo, perishable goods, and time-sensitive shipments find their way through the airport's state-of-the-art logistics systems, further cementing its significance in the global economy.

The seamless connectivity offered by HKG is not just a result of geographic positioning; it is a manifestation of the airport's commitment to innovation and excellence. The terminal design, passenger services, and operational efficiency have been meticulously crafted to ensure a smooth travel experience for passengers navigating a web of connecting flights. The airport's

focus on adopting advanced technologies, such as biometric authentication and digital wayfinding, streamlines the journey and minimizes friction for travelers in transit.

HKG's role as a hub of international travel extends beyond its immediate terminals. The airport's accessibility and connectivity have a profound impact on the tourism industry of Hong Kong and the surrounding regions. The influx of travelers from around the world contributes to the local economy, stimulating sectors such as hospitality, retail, and transportation. Additionally, HKG's role as a hub facilitates business travel, enabling professionals to attend conferences, meetings, and trade events with ease.

For many travelers, HKG is not just a destination in itself but a springboard for exploration. The airport's strategic connections make it possible to seamlessly link diverse destinations and cultures. Travelers can easily combine a visit to Hong Kong's vibrant urban landscape with the tranquility of Bali's beaches or the historic richness of Kyoto. The airport's role as a hub allows for the creation of multi-destination itineraries that encapsulate the diversity of the world.

As the world of travel continues to evolve, so does HKG's role as a hub of international travel. The airport's commitment to innovation, sustainability, and passenger experience positions it as a model for airports of the future. As airlines introduce new routes and expand their networks, HKG adapts to accommodate the changing landscape of travel preferences and trends.

In a world where connections are increasingly vital, Hong Kong International Airport stands as an intersection of dreams and journeys. It is a place where the stories of individual travelers intersect with the narratives of cultures, economies, and societies. Through its global connectivity, HKG enriches the lives of millions, enabling them to explore, connect, and experience the world in ways that only air travel can facilitate.

In conclusion, Hong Kong International Airport's role as a hub of international travel transcends its physical structures and operational systems. It embodies the spirit of human exploration, unity, and exchange. As travelers from diverse backgrounds converge and embark on journeys that span the globe, HKG remains a steadfast facilitator of connections, discovery, and shared experiences. It is a testament to the boundless potential of human mobility and the role that modern airports play in shaping the way we explore our world.

Effortless Transition: Hong Kong International Airport's Seamlessness from Air to Land

In the heart of Hong Kong's dynamic landscape lies an aviation hub that epitomizes the concept of seamless travel—the Hong Kong International Airport (HKG). Beyond its architectural marvels and global connectivity, HKG has mastered the art of facilitating an effortless transition for passengers from the skies to the land. This transition, meticulously designed and executed, encapsulates the airport's commitment to providing an unparalleled travel experience that begins the moment travelers step off the plane.

As passengers disembark from their flights, the transition to land begins with a welcoming environment that reflects the vibrancy and efficiency of Hong Kong. The terminal interiors, designed with aesthetics and functionality in mind, exude a sense of space and light that contrasts the confines of an aircraft cabin. Natural light pours in through expansive windows, offering travelers a glimpse of the city's energy even before they step outside.

Effortless transition also involves accessibility. HKG has incorporated features to accommodate passengers with reduced mobility, ensuring that everyone can navigate the terminal comfortably. From ramps to designated assistance points, the airport's commitment to inclusivity reflects its dedication to a seamless experience for all travelers.

The journey from air to land also involves the intricate choreography of luggage handling. The airport's baggage handling system operates quietly behind the scenes, ensuring that passengers' belongings make their way from the plane to the terminal with minimal delay. Advanced technology and meticulous processes ensure that luggage is efficiently sorted, transferred, and made ready for collection by travelers. This orchestration of efficiency ensures that passengers can continue their journey without worrying about the fate of their checked bags.

Immigration and security procedures are an integral part of the transition process. HKG recognizes the delicate balance between ensuring safety and providing a hassle-free experience for travelers. The adoption of biometric technology and automated immigration kiosks streamlines these processes, allowing passengers to clear customs quickly and efficiently.

The airport's focus on innovation extends to security as well. Advanced screening technologies minimize inconveniences while maintaining stringent security standards. This ensures that the transition from the gate to the city is a smooth and secure one.

One of HKG's most remarkable attributes is its connectivity beyond the terminal doors. Travelers can seamlessly transition from their arrival gates to a range of transportation options that whisk them away to the heart of the city.

The Airport Express, a dedicated train service, offers a quick and comfortable journey to Hong Kong's urban centers. High-speed trains transport passengers to key stations, allowing them to effortlessly access hotels, business districts, and attractions. Additionally, taxis and buses provide further flexibility for those seeking alternative transportation options.

The transition from air to land is not solely about practical matters; it also encompasses the in-between moments that define the travel experience. HKG has masterfully curated an environment that caters to passengers during these moments, ensuring that the transition remains enjoyable and engaging.

The airport's integrated shopping and dining facilities, often referred to as "airports within an airport," offer a range of options that cater to various tastes and preferences. From international brands to local delicacies, travelers can explore a diverse array of offerings as they await their transportation or connect between flights.

Just as the airport orchestrates an effortless transition upon arrival, it ensures the same level of efficiency and service upon departure. The streamlined check-in process, security procedures, and boarding gate arrangements ensure that passengers' journeys conclude with the same seamlessness they experienced upon arrival.

The transition from HKG back to the skies is a bittersweet moment, marked by fond farewells to the city and the anticipation of new beginnings. The airport's role in facilitating these transitions, while seemingly routine, leaves a lasting impression that enriches the overall travel experience.

Hong Kong International Airport's commitment to an effortless transition from air to land goes beyond logistical considerations—it encompasses the ethos of modern travel. The journey from arrival to departure is an integral part of the travel narrative, one that shapes the memories and perceptions travelers carry with them.

In conclusion, the effortless transition from air to land at Hong Kong International Airport is a symphony of design, technology, and hospitality. This transition, marked by seamless processes, innovative solutions, and an inviting environment, is a testament to the airport's commitment to providing an exceptional travel experience. Beyond its utilitarian role, HKG has elevated the concept of transition to an art form, creating an environment where travelers can seamlessly shift between the skies and the city, allowing them to fully immerse themselves in the journey of exploration and discovery.

Innovations in Sustainability: Hong Kong International Airport's Quest for Environmental Excellence

Hong Kong International Airport (HKG) is not merely a transportation hub; it stands as a pioneering exemplar of sustainability within the realm of modern aviation. Beyond its functional prowess and global connectivity, HKG has undertaken a resolute commitment to environmental stewardship. With a visionary approach to sustainable operations, the airport has implemented a spectrum of innovative practices that not only mitigate its environmental impact but also set a benchmark for the aviation industry and beyond.

HKG's journey towards sustainability began with a vision to create an airport that would harmonize with its natural surroundings. Recognizing the significance of its location on Chek

Lap Kok Island—a reclaimed landform—the airport's planners envisioned an integrated facility that would blend seamlessly with the environment. This marked the beginning of a mission to not only reduce the airport's ecological footprint but also to proactively contribute to the conservation and protection of its surroundings.

One of the standout innovations in HKG's sustainability journey is its extensive utilization of solar energy. The airport's terminal buildings and ancillary facilities are adorned with solar panels that harness the power of the sun to generate electricity. These solar installations not only reduce the airport's reliance on conventional power sources but also contribute to the reduction of greenhouse gas emissions, a crucial aspect of combatting climate change.

The adoption of solar energy Is a demonstration of HKG's holistic approach to sustainability, as it aligns with the region's goal to expand its renewable energy capacity and transition towards a low-carbon future.

HKG's commitment to sustainability transcends the installation of solar panels. The airport's terminal buildings are meticulously designed to maximize energy efficiency. Natural light plays a pivotal role in reducing the need for artificial lighting during the day. Skylights, large windows, and innovative architectural elements channel sunlight into the terminal spaces, creating a bright and inviting atmosphere while minimizing energy consumption.

Advanced lighting systems equipped with motion sensors adjust illumination levels based on occupancy, further optimizing energy usage. These innovative design choices reflect the airport's intention to create a sustainable infrastructure that marries aesthetics with functionality.

Innovations in sustainability extend to the way HKG manages its waste. The airport is dedicated to reducing the amount of waste it generates and ensuring that waste materials are managed

responsibly. Recycling initiatives target items such as paper, plastic, glass, and aluminum, diverting these materials from landfills.

Moreover, the airport has embraced the concept of a circular economy by incorporating recycled materials into its infrastructure. For instance, recycled glass is used in construction projects, reducing the demand for virgin resources and minimizing the environmental impact of new construction.

Water scarcity is a global concern, and HKG recognizes the importance of water conservation. The airport employs innovative water-saving technologies that include low-flow fixtures, efficient irrigation systems, and water recycling initiatives. Rainwater harvesting systems collect and store rainwater, which is then used for irrigation and non-potable purposes, further reducing the airport's demand on municipal water sources.

By embracing water-saving technologies, HKG demonstrates its commitment to sustainable water management, aligning with global efforts to address water scarcity and ensure the responsible use of this precious resource.

HKG's innovations in sustainability extend beyond the confines of its terminals. The airport's commitment to green transportation is evident in its efforts to reduce carbon emissions associated with ground transportation. Electric vehicles (EVs) and charging stations are integrated into the airport's fleet, providing an eco-friendly alternative to traditional vehicles. Additionally, the airport encourages passengers and visitors to use environmentally friendly modes of transportation, such as the Airport Express train, to access the facility.

HKG's innovations in sustainability have positioned the airport as a model for the aviation industry and a beacon of inspiration for sustainability initiatives across different sectors. The airport's commitment to sustainability is not an isolated endeavor; it is a reflection of the interconnectedness between responsible business practices, environmental protection, and the well-being of communities.

Innovation in sustainability also extends to educational outreach. HKG actively engages with the public, schools, and visitors to raise awareness about environmental conservation. The airport hosts educational events, workshops, and tours that highlight its sustainability initiatives, aiming to inspire the next generation of environmentally conscious individuals.

In conclusion, Hong Kong International Airport's innovations in sustainability reflect a holistic approach that extends to every facet of its operations. From harnessing solar energy and embracing energy-efficient design to promoting waste reduction and green transportation, the airport serves as a blueprint for sustainable practices within the aviation industry and beyond. HKG's journey is a testament to the power of innovation and dedication, demonstrating that environmental stewardship and operational excellence can coexist to create a brighter and greener future for all.

Sky High Shopping and Dining: SkyPlaza at Hong Kong International Airport

In the heart of Hong Kong International Airport (HKG) lies a destination within a destination—a realm of vibrant shopping, diverse dining, and immersive experiences known as SkyPlaza. Beyond being a mere transit point, HKG's SkyPlaza offers a unique blend of entertainment, culture, and indulgence, making it a haven for travelers seeking respite, excitement, and a taste of Hong Kong's dynamic spirit.

SkyPlaza is more than a shopping and dining complex; it is an embodiment of the city's pulsating energy, showcased through an array of offerings that cater to travelers' every whim. The bustling environment, vibrant ambiance, and diverse experiences transform the transit experience into an adventure in its own right.

SkyPlaza's shopping offerings are a reflection of Hong Kong's reputation as a global retail hub. From luxury brands to local boutiques, travelers are spoiled for choice with an extensive selection of merchandise that spans fashion, accessories, electronics, cosmetics, and more. International travelers can indulge in duty-free shopping, with an assortment of high-end products available at competitive prices.

The retail journey at SkyPlaza extends beyond material acquisitions; it is an exploration of global trends and local craftsmanship. The diverse mix of stores showcases the convergence of cultures and the ever-evolving landscape of consumer preferences. Travelers can discover unique items that encapsulate the essence of their journey through both style and substance.

SkyPlaza's culinary landscape is a gastronomic journey that transcends geographical borders. From local flavors to international cuisines, the dining options cater to diverse palates, offering travelers the opportunity to savor a taste of Hong Kong's culinary prowess.

Restaurants, cafes, and eateries serve up an eclectic range of dishes that mirror the city's multicultural tapestry. Dim sum, a quintessential Hong Kong delight, is available alongside global favorites such as sushi, pasta, and gourmet burgers. Whether travelers are seeking a quick bite or a leisurely dining experience, SkyPlaza's dining scene is a testament to Hong Kong's reputation as a culinary melting pot.

SkyPlaza is more than a retail and dining oasis; it is a canvas for cultural exploration and entertainment. The space often hosts exhibitions, events, and performances that showcase Hong Kong's vibrant arts scene. Travelers can engage with local artists, experience live performances, and interact with installations that celebrate the city's creative spirit.

Interactive displays and exhibitions offer a glimpse into Hong Kong's history, heritage, and contemporary culture. Whether through art installations, music performances, or cultural showcases, SkyPlaza brings the essence of the city to life, allowing travelers to connect with the destination before even setting foot outside the airport.

Traveling can be demanding, and SkyPlaza recognizes the importance of providing travelers with moments of respite. Amid the hustle and bustle of the airport, the complex offers spaces where passengers can relax, unwind, and recharge. Lounges, seating areas, and quiet zones provide a tranquil escape, allowing travelers to catch their breath and prepare for the next leg of their journey.

SkyPlaza's essence encapsulates the vibrant and dynamic spirit of Hong Kong. The complex transcends its role as a mere airport facility; it becomes a microcosm of the city itself. Just as Hong Kong seamlessly blends tradition with innovation, SkyPlaza marries retail, dining, culture, and entertainment to create an immersive experience that resonates with travelers from around the world.

The memories forged within SkyPlaza are an integral part of the travel experience. For some, it might be the thrill of discovering a unique souvenir; for others, it might be the joy of savoring a local delicacy. The interactions, sights, sounds, and flavors become part of travelers' narratives, enriching their connection to Hong Kong.

In conclusion, SkyPlaza at Hong Kong International Airport is not just a space for transit; it is a destination of its own. Through its vibrant retail, diverse dining, cultural engagement, and soothing spaces, SkyPlaza transforms the airport experience into a journey of exploration and enjoyment. It reflects Hong Kong's dynamic essence, offering travelers a preview of the city's spirit and setting the stage for the adventures that await beyond the terminal. As travelers immerse themselves in the offerings of SkyPlaza, they embark on a unique and memorable chapter within their broader travel story.

Beyond Travel: Hong Kong International Airport's Cultural Contribution

Hong Kong International Airport (HKG) is more than a transportation hub; it serves as a gateway not only to the city itself but also to the cultural richness and diversity of the region. Beyond its functional role of facilitating travel, HKG has embraced a broader mission—to contribute to the cultural experience of passengers and visitors. Through art, design, and curated experiences,

the airport has become a platform for cultural exploration, transforming the journey from mere transportation to an enriching voyage of discovery.

The airport experience often marks the beginning or end of a journey, and HKG recognizes the potential for cultural engagement during these pivotal moments. The airport's architectural design itself is an embodiment of Hong Kong's cultural fusion—traditional influences blend seamlessly with modern aesthetics. This synthesis creates an immediate connection between travelers and the cultural ethos of the region.

The presence of art Installations, cultural exhibits, and performances at the airport amplifies this connection, fostering an environment where cultural exploration becomes an integral part of the travel narrative.

HKG has transformed into a living gallery that showcases a diverse range of artworks, sculptures, and installations. These artistic pieces celebrate the heritage of the region, offering travelers a glimpse into the cultural tapestry of Hong Kong and its neighboring areas. From contemporary sculptures to traditional crafts, the airport's corridors and spaces are adorned with visual expressions that capture the essence of the region.

Art installations at HKG often transcend the confines of traditional mediums, engaging travelers through interactive experiences. These installations create moments of introspection, inviting travelers to pause and engage with the cultural narratives that the artworks convey.

The airport's commitment to cultural contribution extends to its curated cultural experiences. Traditional performances, exhibitions, and workshops provide travelers with the opportunity to engage with local traditions and crafts. Traditional dance performances, musical showcases, and demonstrations of cultural practices offer a glimpse into the region's heritage, enriching the travel experience with a deeper understanding of local culture.

Travelers have the chance to participate in workshops that introduce them to local crafts such as calligraphy, tea appreciation, and paper folding. These experiences not only foster cultural appreciation but also empower travelers to create lasting memories and connections with the destination.

HKG serves as a stage for local artists and creators to share their talents with a global audience. Artistic collaborations, exhibitions, and performances provide a platform for emerging and established artists alike to display their work to an international audience. This not only nurtures the local creative ecosystem but also exposes travelers to the vibrancy of the region's artistic scene.

The influence of cultural heritage is not confined to art installations; it is embedded in the airport's architectural design and interior spaces. Elements of Hong Kong's cultural identity are woven into the fabric of the airport, from design motifs that pay homage to local crafts to

architectural details that reference historical landmarks. This attention to design serves as a constant reminder of the rich cultural heritage that the airport represents.

HKG's cultural contribution transcends the surface-level experience of travel. It transforms the journey from being a mere transportation process to an exploration of identity, diversity, and interconnectedness. Travelers are not just moving from one place to another; they are engaging with the narratives of cultures, traditions, and artistic expressions that shape the destinations they visit.

The airport's commitment to cultural contribution also facilitates a global exchange of cultures. Travelers from diverse backgrounds are exposed to the rich tapestry of the region's heritage, fostering understanding and appreciation. This intercultural interaction creates a microcosm of global unity within the airport's walls, where individuals from different corners of the world share moments of cultural exchange.

In conclusion, Hong Kong International Airport's cultural contribution goes beyond the utilitarian role of facilitating travel; it embodies the power of culture to transform the travel experience. Through art, design, performances, and curated experiences, the airport serves as a conduit for cultural immersion, understanding, and connection. As travelers pass through its terminals, they are not only embarking on journeys of exploration but also embarking on journeys of cultural discovery that enrich their lives and broaden their perspectives.

Memories in Every Departure: Hong Kong International Airport's Profound Impact

As the beating heart of international travel, Hong Kong International Airport (HKG) is more than a point of departure; it is a portal to the world, a conduit of dreams, and a repository of memories. Within its sprawling terminals, bustling gates, and welcoming lounges, HKG weaves a tapestry of experiences that transcend the act of traveling itself. With every departure, the airport leaves an indelible mark on the hearts and minds of travelers, imparting memories that linger long after the journey has ended.

Departures are poignant moments that evoke a whirlwind of emotions. The airport serves as the stage for farewells and reunions, a backdrop to bittersweet moments as loved ones bid adieu or embrace after long separations. It is within these emotions that the airport's profound impact is most keenly felt.

HKG's departure halls become a canvas for human stories—each traveler carries a narrative, a purpose, and a destination. The airport, in its role as a facilitator of these stories, becomes woven into the fabric of travelers' memories, forever connected to the emotions experienced during these pivotal moments.

For many, the airport is a threshold where dreams take flight. It is a place of transformation where individuals embark on journeys of discovery, growth, and self-discovery. Whether it's a student leaving for an overseas education, an entrepreneur seeking new business opportunities, or an adventurer setting out to explore uncharted territories, the airport represents the realization of aspirations.

The act of departing from HKG becomes a symbol of courage, determination, and ambition. The airport stands as a silent witness to these aspirations, an integral chapter in the stories of countless individuals who dare to chase their dreams.

HKG's impact transcends geographic boundaries. As a global crossroads, the airport brings together cultures, languages, and traditions from around the world. Departure gates become meeting points for travelers from diverse backgrounds, converging in a shared moment before dispersing to their respective destinations.

This cultural fusion imprints a unique sense of unity and interconnectedness in travelers' memories. The airport's multicultural environment encourages interactions and exchanges, leaving travelers with lasting impressions of the rich tapestry of humanity.

Departure areas also offer moments of solitude and reflection. As travelers wait for their flights, they have the opportunity to pause and contemplate. Whether gazing out at the tarmac, enjoying a cup of coffee, or simply observing the hustle and bustle of fellow passengers, these moments become an integral part of the travel experience.

Within these spaces of reflection, the airport imparts a sense of serenity and contemplation. Travelers may find themselves pondering the journey ahead, reminiscing about the one just concluded, or savoring the anticipation of reuniting with loved ones at the destination.

HKG's architecture and design play a significant role in shaping travelers' memories. The terminal's aesthetic elements, such as its sweeping lines, abundant natural light, and immersive art installations, contribute to the overall ambiance of departure. These visual cues create a distinct atmosphere that lingers in travelers' memories, becoming synonymous with their departure experience.

The architectural brilliance of the airport transforms departures into more than just a logistical process; it becomes an aesthetic journey that evokes emotions and captures moments in time.

Departures from HKG mark not just an end but a continuation. They signify a transition from one chapter to the next, a dynamic evolution in the lives of travelers. The airport, in this sense, becomes a thread that weaves together the narrative of individual journeys.

As travelers depart from HKG, they carry with them not only their luggage but a treasure trove of memories—moments of joy, anticipation, reflection, and connection. These memories serve as a testament to the airport's profound impact, its role as a catalyst for experiences, and its status as a keeper of tales from every departure.

In conclusion, Hong Kong International Airport's impact transcends its functional role as a transportation hub. It reaches into the realms of emotion, aspiration, and cultural exchange, imprinting memories on travelers' hearts and minds with every departure. The airport's ability to evoke emotions, foster connections, and symbolize journeys makes it an integral part of the travel experience—an enduring presence in the memories of those who pass through its gates. As travelers take their leave, HKG leaves behind an everlasting imprint, a reminder of the transformative power of travel and the cherished memories that accompany every departure.

B. Shenzhen Bao'an International Airport (SZX): Connecting the Pearl River Delta and Beyond

Nestled within the bustling metropolis of Shenzhen, China, Shenzhen Bao'an International Airport (SZX) stands as a pivotal hub of air travel in the Pearl River Delta region. Renowned for its modern facilities, efficient operations, and strategic location, SZX plays a crucial role in connecting travelers from both domestic and international destinations. As a gateway to the economic and technological powerhouse that is Shenzhen, the airport's impact extends beyond its runways and terminals, shaping the region's development and global connectivity.

Strategic Location: A Nexus of Growth

SZX's strategic location is central to its significance. Situated in close proximity to the Pearl River Delta's key urban centers, the airport serves as a catalyst for economic growth and urban development. Shenzhen, known as China's "Silicon Valley," is a hub of innovation, technology, and manufacturing. SZX's accessibility supports the city's position as a global leader in these sectors, facilitating the movement of professionals, entrepreneurs, and investors.

Additionally, SZX's proximity to Hong Kong—a mere stone's throw away via various transportation options—further enhances the airport's regional connectivity and its role as an

integral component of the Greater Bay Area, a cluster of cities with immense economic potential.

Efficient Operations: Seamless Travel Experience

Efficiency is at the heart of SZX's operations. The airport's modern infrastructure and state-of-the-art facilities are designed to provide travelers with a seamless and convenient journey.

From check-in and security procedures to baggage handling and boarding, SZX's commitment to operational excellence ensures that passengers can navigate the airport with ease.

The airport's efficient operations are also reflected in its ability to accommodate a high volume of flights and passengers. SZX ranks among the busiest airports in the world, a testament to its capacity to manage the demands of both domestic and international air travel.

Global Connectivity: Bridging Cultures and Economies

SZX's impact extends beyond its immediate surroundings. The airport's extensive network of routes connects travelers from across the globe, facilitating the exchange of cultures, ideas, and economies. As China's economic influence grows, SZX serves as a vital gateway for international business travelers, diplomats, and tourists seeking to explore the country's dynamic landscape.

The airport's international connections not only boost tourism and trade but also enhance Shenzhen's reputation as an international city. Through SZX, Shenzhen welcomes a diverse array of visitors who contribute to the city's vibrancy and global appeal.

Gateway to Shenzhen: Exploring Innovation and Culture

SZX is more than a transport hub; it is a window into Shenzhen's unique blend of innovation and culture. The airport's design elements and interior spaces reflect the city's commitment to modernity and creativity. Art installations, cultural exhibitions, and design aesthetics serve as an introduction to the city's identity, inviting travelers to explore Shenzhen's bustling streets, tech parks, and cultural landmarks.

For international visitors, SZX acts as a portal to a city that seamlessly fuses traditional Chinese heritage with cutting-edge technology. As travelers venture beyond the airport, they can immerse themselves in Shenzhen's vibrant cultural scene, experience its renowned electronics markets, and witness the tangible effects of its rapid urban development.

Economic Engine: Facilitating Trade and Investment

SZX's impact on Shenzhen's economy is palpable. The airport's connectivity enhances the city's status as an economic powerhouse, attracting businesses and investment from around the world. SZX's efficient cargo facilities facilitate the movement of goods, serving as a conduit for trade and commerce that supports Shenzhen's industrial sectors.

Additionally, SZX's connectivity complements the city's efforts to develop free trade zones and special economic zones, further positioning Shenzhen as a magnet for international trade and investment.

A Hub of Innovation and Progress

As China continues to evolve and shape the global landscape, Shenzhen Bao'an International Airport stands as a microcosm of this progress. It embodies China's ambition, innovation, and connectivity as it navigates the complexities of modern air travel and international relations. The airport's growth trajectory reflects not only China's economic rise but also its role as a hub of cultural exchange, technological advancement, and global integration.

The Gateway to Opportunity

In conclusion, Shenzhen Bao'an International Airport is much more than a transportation node; it is a gateway to opportunity. Its strategic location, efficient operations, and global connectivity position it as a dynamic center that facilitates economic growth, cultural exchange, and international collaboration. Through its terminals, Shenzhen's spirit of innovation and progress comes to life, inviting travelers to explore a city that thrives at the intersection of tradition and modernity. As travelers pass through SZX, they embark on a journey that not only connects destinations but also bridges cultures, fosters understanding, and opens doors to new horizons.

Strategic Location: Shenzhen Bao'an International Airport's Nexus of Growth

Shenzhen Bao'an International Airport (SZX) stands as a beacon of connectivity and progress, strategically positioned at the heart of the bustling metropolis of Shenzhen, China. Its location is not just a matter of geography; it's a powerful driver of economic growth, technological

innovation, and urban development that radiates across the Pearl River Delta region and beyond. As a nexus of growth, SZX's strategic location has played a pivotal role in shaping Shenzhen's transformation from a humble fishing village to a global hub of trade, technology, and opportunity.

Shenzhen's rise from a small fishing village to a sprawling megacity is a testament to the transformative power of strategic location. Located adjacent to Hong Kong, Shenzhen's proximity to this global financial hub provided the city with a unique opportunity to leverage Hong Kong's global connections, business acumen, and expertise.

Shenzhen's strategic location near major sea routes, along with the establishment of special economic zones in the 1980s, attracted foreign investment, international trade, and technological innovation. As Shenzhen embraced its role as a gateway to China's manufacturing prowess, the city's landscape transformed rapidly, giving birth to modern skyscrapers, research centers, and industrial parks.

Shenzhen's strategic location also catalyzed its emergence as a global technology powerhouse. The city's proximity to Hong Kong's financial resources and international networks allowed it to attract talent, investment, and ideas from around the world. This influx of knowledge and capital laid the foundation for a vibrant ecosystem of innovation and entrepreneurship.

As SZX became a gateway to this technological playground, it facilitated the movement of professionals, researchers, and investors who flocked to Shenzhen's tech parks and research institutions. The airport's location bridged the gap between research and market, providing a seamless conduit for ideas to transform into products and services.

Strategic location is often synonymous with economic prosperity, and SZX's position has amplified Shenzhen's economic prowess. The airport's close proximity to major manufacturing centers, global markets, and trading partners has positioned the city as a key player in global trade.

As Shenzhen developed into a manufacturing hub, SZX's cargo facilities played a vital role in facilitating the movement of goods. The airport's efficient logistics systems and direct connections to international destinations allowed businesses to efficiently import and export products, contributing to Shenzhen's economic boom.

SZX's strategic location has not only fueled local growth but has also transformed Shenzhen into an international hub. The airport's proximity to Hong Kong, coupled with its extensive network of routes, has made Shenzhen an attractive destination for global business travelers, tourists, and diplomats. SZX's role as a gateway to mainland China has amplified Shenzhen's visibility on the world stage.

The airport's International connectivity has also supported Shenzhen's efforts to attract foreign investment and forge international partnerships. The ease of travel provided by SZX has made it convenient for businesses and investors to explore opportunities within the city, thereby contributing to Shenzhen's status as a global city of significance.

Beyond Shenzhen's borders, SZX's strategic location has also influenced the broader urban dynamics of the Pearl River Delta. The airport's accessibility has facilitated the growth of surrounding cities and regions by providing efficient transportation links to Shenzhen's economic and technological centers.

The development of transportation networks, such as high-speed rail and road connections, has enhanced the integration of cities within the region. SZX's strategic location serves as a linchpin in this network, making it possible for people, goods, and ideas to flow seamlessly between different urban centers.

In conclusion, Shenzhen Bao'an International Airport's strategic location goes beyond its physical coordinates—it represents a nexus of growth, innovation, and connectivity. Its proximity to major economic, technological, and cultural centers has elevated Shenzhen's status on the global stage. As SZX serves as a gateway to Shenzhen's economic opportunities, technological advancements, and cultural richness, it embodies the city's journey from a modest fishing village to a dynamic global city.

The airport's strategic location has positioned Shenzhen as a bridge between the past and the future, tradition and innovation, and local and global. As the world continues to evolve, SZX's significance as a nexus of growth will continue to shape Shenzhen's trajectory, amplifying its influence and impact on the world stage.

Efficient Operations: Shenzhen Bao'an International Airport's Commitment to Seamless Travel

Efficiency is the cornerstone of an exceptional travel experience, and Shenzhen Bao'an International Airport (SZX) has mastered the art of seamless operations. With its state-of-the-art facilities, streamlined processes, and commitment to passenger satisfaction, SZX has redefined the airport journey. From the moment travelers step through its doors to the time they board their flights, SZX's dedication to efficiency transforms travel into a smooth, stress-free, and enjoyable endeavor.

Efficient operations begin with streamlined processes that optimize every step of the airport journey. SZX's check-in procedures, security screenings, and baggage handling systems are designed to minimize waiting times and maximize passenger convenience. The use of advanced technology, automated check-in kiosks, and self-service options empowers travelers to navigate the airport at their own pace, reducing queues and bottlenecks.

The airport's commitment to real-time information updates ensures that passengers are well-informed about flight statuses, gate changes, and other crucial details. This transparency empowers travelers to make informed decisions and adjust their plans accordingly, enhancing their overall experience.

Technology lies at the heart of SZX's efficient operations. The airport's integration of cutting-edge systems and innovations streamlines processes and reduces manual intervention. Automated bag drop stations, biometric identification, and electronic boarding passes minimize friction, allowing passengers to move seamlessly from one stage of their journey to the next.

Moreover, the implementation of smart airport concepts, such as IoT (Internet of Things) devices and data analytics, enables SZX to monitor passenger flows, optimize resource allocation, and identify potential areas for improvement. This data-driven approach ensures that the airport can adapt to evolving passenger needs and enhance operational efficiency.

Efficient operations at SZX are not just about individual processes; they extend to managing a high volume of flights and passengers. As one of the busiest airports in the world, SZX has fine-tuned its operations to accommodate a significant influx of travelers without compromising on quality.

The airport's design and infrastructure are optimized for passenger flow, minimizing congestion and allowing travelers to move smoothly through terminals. The coordination of ground services, baggage handling, and aircraft turnaround times exemplifies SZX's commitment to maintaining operational excellence, even in the face of high demand.

Efficiency at SZX is not just a technical goal; it's a commitment to providing a customer-centric experience. The airport's staff is trained to prioritize passenger satisfaction, offering assistance and guidance whenever needed. From providing directions to facilitating seamless connections, SZX's personnel contribute to the overall efficiency of the travel experience.

Additionally, SZX's dedication to passenger comfort is evident in its well-designed waiting areas, lounges, and amenities. Travelers can find relaxation zones, charging stations, and comfortable seating options, all designed to enhance their experience while waiting for their flights.

Efficiency at SZX extends beyond passenger travel; it encompasses cargo operations as well. The airport's cargo facilities are equipped with advanced technology and processes that expedite the movement of goods. From perishable items to high-value products, SZX's cargo operations ensure that shipments reach their destinations promptly and in optimal condition.

SZX's cargo efficiency plays a crucial role in supporting Shenzhen's status as a global manufacturing and trading hub. The airport's ability to efficiently handle imports and exports contributes to the city's economic growth and global influence.

In conclusion, Shenzhen Bao'an International Airport's commitment to efficient operations transforms the airport experience into a seamless journey of possibilities. From technology integration and streamlined processes to operational excellence and a customer-centric approach, every facet of SZX's operations is designed to enhance traveler satisfaction.

The airport's efficiency goes beyond mere convenience; it enables travelers to focus on their journey's purpose, whether it's exploring new destinations, conducting business, or reuniting with loved ones. As SZX continues to embrace technological advancements and refine its processes, its efficient operations will serve as a benchmark for airports worldwide, setting the standard for excellence in providing a truly seamless travel experience.

Global Connectivity: Shenzhen Bao'an International Airport's Bridge of Cultures and Economies

Shenzhen Bao'an International Airport (SZX) is not just a physical infrastructure; it is a nexus of connections that transcend geographical boundaries, bridging cultures, economies, and aspirations. As a gateway to the world, SZX plays a pivotal role in global connectivity, facilitating the exchange of ideas, goods, and experiences. With its extensive network of routes and commitment to international collaboration, the airport serves as a bridge that fosters understanding, drives economic growth, and enriches the lives of millions.

At the heart of global connectivity is the exchange of cultures. SZX's vast network of international flights welcomes travelers from diverse backgrounds, each carrying their unique stories, traditions, and perspectives. The airport becomes a microcosm of the world, where people from different corners of the globe converge, share experiences, and forge connections.

These interactions serve as catalysts for cultural exchange and understanding. As travelers from different cultures intermingle within the airport's terminals, they have the opportunity to engage, learn, and appreciate the richness of global diversity. SZX becomes a stage for cross-cultural encounters, creating moments that enrich the human experience and bridge cultural gaps.

Global connectivity is a cornerstone of international trade and economic growth. SZX's extensive network of routes links Shenzhen to cities around the world, enabling the seamless movement of goods and services. The airport's cargo facilities play a critical role in supporting Shenzhen's status as a global manufacturing hub.

Through SZX, Shenzhen's businesses gain access to international markets, and foreign companies find a gateway to China's vast consumer base. The airport's connectivity encourages trade, attracts investment, and contributes to the economic vibrancy of the region. SZX's role in global connectivity extends beyond its runways; it fuels the engine of economic prosperity.

Global connectivity is not confined to physical goods—it extends to the exchange of knowledge, ideas, and innovations. SZX's role in connecting Shenzhen to the world plays a crucial role in technology transfer and collaboration. The airport becomes a conduit through which researchers, scientists, and professionals from various fields share insights, expertise, and breakthroughs.

Shenzhen's reputation as a technological powerhouse is amplified by SZX's ability to attract global experts and innovators. Through international partnerships and collaborations, the airport contributes to the city's innovation ecosystem, fostering the exchange of ideas that drive technological advancements and shape the future.

Global connectivity extends to the realm of cultural diplomacy. SZX serves as a platform for showcasing Shenzhen's identity and values to the world. The airport's design, art installations, and cultural exhibitions offer glimpses into the city's heritage, innovation, and creative spirit. Travelers passing through SZX gain insights into Shenzhen's past, present, and aspirations for the future.

Cultural diplomacy facilitated by the airport's connectivity enhances Shenzhen's global reputation and influence. The city's commitment to creativity, progress, and open-mindedness is communicated to the world through the experiences offered within the airport's terminals.

Global connectivity also plays a transformative role in the realm of tourism and personal experiences. SZX's network of international flights opens doors to new destinations, enabling travelers to explore new cultures, landmarks, and landscapes. The airport becomes a catalyst for personal growth, broadening horizons and enriching lives through immersive travel experiences.

Through SZX, travelers embark on journeys that extend beyond sightseeing; they engage with local communities, learn from different perspectives, and create memories that last a lifetime. The airport's role in connecting people to new horizons fosters a sense of curiosity, empathy, and appreciation for the world's diversity.

In conclusion, Shenzhen Bao'an International Airport's commitment to global connectivity transcends the act of flying—it represents a bridge that unites cultures, economies, and individuals. The airport's extensive network of routes fosters cultural exchange, economic integration, technological advancement, and personal enrichment. As SZX connects Shenzhen to the world, it becomes a symbol of unity, understanding, and progress.

Through the connections facilitated by SZX, Shenzhen's aspirations and achievements resonate across continents. The airport's role as a bridge of cultures and economies underscores the transformative power of travel, reminding us that every journey undertaken is a step toward building a more interconnected, inclusive, and vibrant world.

Gateway to Shenzhen: Shenzhen Bao'an International Airport's Exploration of Innovation and Culture

Shenzhen Bao'an International Airport (SZX) stands as more than just an entry point; it is a gateway that offers travelers a captivating introduction to the dynamic fusion of innovation and culture that defines Shenzhen, China. Nestled in the heart of this technological epicenter, SZX serves as a microcosm of the city's identity, welcoming visitors with a myriad of experiences that showcase Shenzhen's remarkable journey from a fishing village to a global hub of innovation, creativity, and culture.

From the moment travelers step into SZX's terminals, they are greeted by an architectural marvel that reflects Shenzhen's forward-thinking spirit. The airport's design seamlessly integrates modern aesthetics with functional efficiency, mirroring the city's commitment to innovation and progress.

Bold geometric shapes, sleek lines, and abundant natural light create an ambiance that resonates with Shenzhen's technological prowess. Every corner of the airport exudes a sense of innovation, inviting travelers to embark on a journey that mirrors the city's own transformation from humble origins to a global innovation powerhouse.

SZX is more than a transportation hub; it is a canvas that brings art to life. The airport's terminals are adorned with immersive art installations that tell stories of Shenzhen's evolution and cultural vibrancy. From interactive sculptures to multimedia exhibits, each piece reflects the city's creative energy and willingness to embrace experimentation.

These art installations serve as an introduction to the city's artistic scene, offering travelers a glimpse into the cultural fusion that defines Shenzhen. They serve as visual narratives that capture the essence of the city's journey, from its origins as a fishing village to its current status as a global center of innovation.

Shenzhen's identity is a harmonious blend of tradition and modernity, and SZX encapsulates this duality through its cultural showcases. Travelers are treated to exhibitions that celebrate the city's rich history, traditions, and contemporary achievements. These showcases offer a lens through which visitors can explore Shenzhen's transformation into a city that balances its cultural heritage with its thirst for progress.

Traditional artifacts, innovative designs, and technological breakthroughs coexist within the airport's spaces, offering travelers a taste of Shenzhen's multi-dimensional identity. From calligraphy displays to showcases of cutting-edge electronics, these cultural exhibits paint a comprehensive picture of the city's journey.

Innovation is not limited to technology—it extends to culinary experiences that push boundaries and redefine traditional flavors. SZX's dining options offer a culinary adventure that mirrors Shenzhen's innovative spirit. Travelers can savor a diverse range of cuisines, from local delicacies that celebrate the city's culinary heritage to international offerings that reflect its global outlook.

The airport's dining spaces become platforms for exploring the city's gastronomic landscape. As travelers indulge in innovative dishes and fusion flavors, they are reminded that Shenzhen's penchant for innovation extends to every aspect of life, including its culinary arts.

SZX transforms waiting periods into opportunities for engagement through its interactive zones. These spaces allow travelers to experience Shenzhen's technological advancements firsthand. Interactive displays, virtual reality experiences, and augmented reality installations create immersive environments that showcase the city's achievements in fields such as electronics, robotics, and artificial intelligence.

By inviting travelers to participate in these interactive zones, SZX offers a taste of Shenzhen's culture of experimentation and innovation. These experiences not only entertain but also educate, leaving a lasting impression of Shenzhen's technological prowess.

In conclusion, Shenzhen Bao'an International Airport is more than a gateway; it is a curtain-raiser to the city's captivating narrative of innovation and culture. The airport's architecture, art installations, cultural showcases, culinary offerings, and interactive zones together encapsulate the essence of Shenzhen's transformation.

As travelers pass through SZX's terminals, they are not merely embarking on journeys; they are embarking on an exploration of Shenzhen's spirit. The airport serves as a microcosm of the city's ability to merge tradition and modernity, to embrace innovation while cherishing its roots. In this way, SZX extends an invitation to all who pass through its gates—an invitation to discover the vibrant, ever-evolving city of Shenzhen and to become a part of its ongoing story of progress and culture.

Economic Engine: Shenzhen Bao'an International Airport's Role in Facilitating Trade and Investment

Shenzhen Bao'an International Airport (SZX) is not merely a transportation hub; it is a vital economic engine that powers Shenzhen's global trade, investment, and industrial growth. Situated at the crossroads of domestic and international connectivity, SZX plays a pivotal role in driving economic prosperity by facilitating the movement of goods, fostering trade relationships, and attracting foreign investment. As a gateway to Shenzhen's economic opportunities, the airport serves as a catalyst for economic transformation, positioning the city as a dynamic global player in the realm of trade and commerce.

SZX's strategic location within the Pearl River Delta and its extensive network of international flights position it as a gateway to global markets. The airport's connectivity enables businesses in Shenzhen to access markets around the world with remarkable ease. The seamless flow of goods from production centers to the airport's cargo facilities ensures that Shenzhen's products can reach consumers on a global scale.

This global gateway status enhances the competitiveness of Shenzhen's industries, allowing them to capitalize on international demand and remain agile in a rapidly evolving global market. SZX's role as an economic engine is evident in its ability to bridge the gap between local industries and the international marketplace.

Efficient cargo operations are at the heart of SZX's economic impact. The airport's state-of-the-art cargo facilities, advanced technology, and streamlined processes expedite the movement of goods, ensuring that they reach their destinations promptly and efficiently. From perishable goods to high-value electronics, SZX's cargo operations cater to a diverse range of industries.

As Shenzhen has evolved into a global manufacturing hub, SZX's cargo facilities have played a crucial role in supporting the city's export-oriented industries. The airport's commitment to efficient cargo operations enhances Shenzhen's competitive advantage, allowing businesses to maintain their global supply chains and meet customer demands with precision.

SZX's global connectivity fosters international trade relations that go beyond physical goods. The airport becomes a hub of business interactions, enabling entrepreneurs, investors, and professionals to converge and engage in meaningful collaborations. Business travelers passing through SZX engage in networking, negotiation, and relationship-building that have the potential to drive economic growth and innovation.

The airport's role in facilitating face-to-face meetings enhances trust, transparency, and communication among global business partners. As Shenzhen aims to diversify its economy and expand its industries, SZX's role as a catalyst for international trade relations becomes increasingly significant.

Shenzhen's position as a global economic powerhouse is augmented by SZX's ability to attract foreign investment. The airport acts as a welcoming gateway that showcases Shenzhen's potential as an investment destination. Foreign investors arriving at SZX are greeted with a city that boasts a vibrant ecosystem of innovation, a favorable business environment, and a strong foundation for growth.

As SZX facilitates the movement of foreign investors and business delegations, it amplifies Shenzhen's attractiveness as a hub for innovation, technology, and commerce. The airport becomes a first impression that resonates with potential investors, encouraging them to explore the city's numerous investment opportunities.

Shenzhen's designation as a special economic zone has significantly contributed to its economic success, and SZX plays a role in enabling this growth. The airport connects Shenzhen's special economic zones to global markets, serving as a conduit for raw materials, components, and finished goods. SZX's proximity to these zones enhances their efficiency and effectiveness, propelling Shenzhen's economic development.

Moreover, SZX's connectivity extends beyond Shenzhen's borders, benefiting neighboring regions as well. The airport's accessibility supports the growth of surrounding areas, contributing to the broader economic prosperity of the Pearl River Delta.

In conclusion, Shenzhen Bao'an International Airport's role as an economic engine is a testament to its significance as more than a transportation hub. The airport's efficient cargo operations, facilitation of international trade relations, and ability to attract foreign investment all contribute to Shenzhen's economic growth trajectory. As the city continues to evolve, SZX will remain a driving force that empowers businesses, fosters economic partnerships, and positions Shenzhen as a global economic powerhouse.

Through its role in facilitating trade and investment, SZX shapes Shenzhen's future as a city that thrives on innovation, embraces globalization, and champions economic growth. The airport's impact extends far beyond its runways, leaving an indelible mark on Shenzhen's economic landscape and solidifying its status as a beacon of opportunity in the global arena.

A Hub of Innovation and Progress: Shenzhen Bao'an International Airport's Role in Shaping the Future

Shenzhen Bao'an International Airport (SZX) is not only a gateway to a city of innovation and progress; it embodies these qualities itself. Situated at the heart of Shenzhen, China's technological epicenter, SZX serves as a hub that encapsulates the city's spirit of innovation, experimentation, and relentless pursuit of progress. From its cutting-edge design to its incorporation of advanced technology, the airport's very essence resonates with Shenzhen's identity as a city that continually pushes boundaries, redefines norms, and shapes the future.

The moment travelers step foot into SZX's terminals, they are greeted by an architectural marvel that reflects Shenzhen's unwavering commitment to innovation. The airport's design seamlessly integrates modern aesthetics with functional efficiency, mirroring the city's approach to innovation, where form and function coalesce seamlessly.

Bold geometric shapes, sleek lines, and expansive spaces create an ambiance that resonates with Shenzhen's technological prowess. Just as the city's skyline is dotted with futuristic skyscrapers, SZX's architecture stands as a testament to Shenzhen's innovative vision. The airport becomes a physical manifestation of the city's evolution from a fishing village to a global technological powerhouse.

Innovation is woven into the very fabric of SZX's operations. The airport leverages cutting-edge technology to enhance every aspect of the traveler's journey. Automated check-in kiosks, biometric identification systems, and smart boarding procedures streamline the passenger experience, exemplifying Shenzhen's pioneering approach to integrating technology for seamless efficiency.

Moreover, SZX's commitment to technological excellence extends to its cargo operations. Advanced tracking systems, automated warehousing, and real-time data analytics optimize the movement of goods, contributing to Shenzhen's reputation as a global manufacturing and trading hub.

SZX goes beyond traditional airport experiences by creating interactive zones that engage and educate travelers. These spaces are designed to showcase Shenzhen's technological advancements, allowing passengers to explore virtual reality exhibits, experience augmented reality installations, and interact with displays that highlight the city's innovations.

These interactive experiences mirror Shenzhen's culture of curiosity, experimentation, and exploration. By inviting travelers to participate in these engaging encounters, SZX ignites a spark of wonder and encourages individuals to embrace the city's innovative spirit.

Innovation in Shenzhen is not confined to technology; it extends to the city's unique blend of tradition and modernity. SZX serves as a microcosm of this cultural fusion, where travelers can experience a harmonious symphony of old and new. The airport's design, art installations, and cultural showcases reflect Shenzhen's ability to honor its cultural heritage while embracing progress.

Traditional Chinese aesthetics are seamlessly intertwined with contemporary design elements, creating an environment that resonates with Shenzhen's ethos. Just as the city's streets are lined with ancient temples and high-tech buildings, SZX captures the essence of Shenzhen's dual identity and serves as a testament to the city's capacity to balance tradition with innovation.

In conclusion, Shenzhen Bao'an International Airport is not only a hub of innovation and progress; it is a symbol of Shenzhen's aspirations and legacy. The airport's architectural marvel, technological integration, interactive experiences, and cultural fusion collectively encapsulate Shenzhen's remarkable journey.

Just as Shenzhen transforms the present into the future, SZX stands as a testament to the city's vision of what is possible. It is a tangible representation of Shenzhen's ability to adapt, innovate, and lead in an ever-changing world. As travelers pass through SZX's terminals, they are reminded that the city's pursuit of innovation is not limited to labs and factories—it extend to every corner of its vibrant landscape.

Ultimately, SZX's role as a hub of innovation and progress underscores Shenzhen's status as a city that shapes the future. The airport is more than a physical infrastructure; it is an embodiment of the city's unwavering commitment to pushing boundaries, embracing change, and pioneering the path toward new horizons. In this way, SZX continues to stand as a beacon of inspiration for both travelers and the city it represents.

The Gateway to Opportunity: Shenzhen Bao'an International Airport's Role in Paving Pathways to Success

Shenzhen Bao'an International Airport (SZX) serves as more than a transit point; it is a gateway to a world of opportunity that beckons travelers to explore, discover, and realize their

aspirations. Positioned in the heart of Shenzhen, China's thriving technological and economic hub, SZX embodies the city's ethos of progress, innovation, and limitless potential. From its strategic location to its role in facilitating business ventures, education, and cultural exchanges, the airport opens doors to a universe of possibilities, transforming journeys into transformative experiences that lead to success.

SZX's strategic location at the epicenter of Shenzhen's economic and technological prowess plays a pivotal role in its status as the gateway to opportunity. Positioned adjacent to some of the world's most influential cities, including Hong Kong, SZX enjoys unparalleled connectivity to global markets, financial centers, and innovation hubs.

The airport's proximity to these strategic locations enhances Shenzhen's competitive edge, allowing businesses, entrepreneurs, and investors to tap into a network that spans continents. As travelers disembark at SZX, they step into a world brimming with opportunities, where connections to innovation and growth are just a flight away.

For ambitious individuals and visionary entrepreneurs, SZX is not just an airport; it's the starting point of a journey toward business success. Shenzhen's status as a global tech hub attracts innovators from around the world, and SZX serves as their first introduction to a city that embraces disruption, experimentation, and transformative ideas.

The airport's connectivity and accessibility are vital for business travelers seeking to explore partnerships, attend industry events, or initiate collaborations. As they step onto Shenzhen's soil through SZX, these entrepreneurs enter an ecosystem where dreams are transformed into reality, and innovation is cultivated with unmatched enthusiasm.

SZX is not only a gateway to Shenzhen's bustling business environment; it also opens doors to educational opportunities that fuel personal growth and intellectual advancement. The city's reputation as a technological powerhouse attracts scholars, researchers, and students in pursuit of knowledge and innovation.

The airport's role in connecting academia to the city's research institutions and universities contributes to the exchange of ideas and expertise. As students and researchers pass through SZX, they enter a world where learning is inextricably linked to real-world applications, offering them a chance to be part of Shenzhen's educational ecosystem and contribute to its ongoing progress.

Opportunities extended by SZX transcend business and education—they encompass cultural enrichment as well. Shenzhen's global status is mirrored in the diversity of its residents and visitors, each contributing their unique cultural perspectives to the city's dynamic tapestry. SZX serves as the entry point for these cultural exchanges, inviting travelers to immerse themselves in Shenzhen's cosmopolitan atmosphere.

Cultural events, exhibitions, and performances within the airport's terminals create an environment where cross-cultural interactions become the norm. As travelers experience Shenzhen's cultural fusion, they become part of a global dialogue that celebrates diversity and fosters mutual understanding.

In conclusion, Shenzhen Bao'an International Airport's role as the gateway to opportunity is not just a tagline—it is a testament to its transformative impact. The airport's strategic location, its facilitation of business ventures, its role in education and research, and its promotion of cultural exchange collectively contribute to Shenzhen's status as a city of limitless possibilities.

SZX serves as a catalyst for transformation, turning aspirations into achievements, and dreams into reality. For the businessperson seeking innovation, the student pursuing knowledge, the artist exploring creativity, and the traveler embarking on a new adventure, SZX becomes the gateway to a world where potential knows no bounds.

As travelers arrive at SZX and embark on their journeys through the city's bustling streets, innovation hubs, and cultural enclaves, they carry with them the spirit of possibility that the airport embodies. In this way, SZX continues to shape Shenzhen's narrative as a city that opens doors, unlocks potential, and inspires the world to seize the countless opportunities that await beyond its gates.

II.   Transportation within the City

Navigating a bustling metropolis like Shenzhen requires efficient and reliable transportation options. Fortunately, the city boasts a comprehensive transportation network that caters to various preferences and needs. From modern metro systems to convenient buses and emerging ride-sharing services, Shenzhen offers a range of transportation choices that ensure residents and visitors can move seamlessly across the city.

Metro System: The Backbone of Shenzhen's Transportation

The Shenzhen Metro is the backbone of the city's transportation system. It is known for its extensive coverage, efficiency, and cleanliness. The metro network comprises multiple lines that connect key areas, commercial centers, residential neighborhoods, and tourist attractions. The trains are punctual and offer a cost-effective way to travel around Shenzhen.

The metro system is complemented by modern stations equipped with clear signage, digital displays, and security measures. It is an excellent choice for both daily commuters and tourists exploring the city's landmarks and districts.

Buses: Comprehensive Coverage

Shenzhen's bus system provides comprehensive coverage, reaching areas that may not be directly accessible by the metro. The city's bus network is extensive, with a variety of routes that serve different parts of the city. Buses offer a budget-friendly mode of transportation and allow passengers to enjoy scenic views while traveling.

While the bus system can be slightly more challenging for non-Chinese speakers due to limited English signage, smartphone apps and route maps can assist travelers in navigating the system effectively.

Taxis: Convenience and Flexibility

Taxis are a convenient and flexible option for travelers seeking personalized transportation. Shenzhen's taxis are readily available and offer air-conditioned comfort, making them a popular choice during hot summer months. Most taxi drivers in major areas understand basic English phrases, making communication relatively easy.

It's advisable to have your destination written in Chinese characters to ensure smooth communication with the driver. Taxis can be hailed on the street or booked through ride-hailing apps like Didi, which also provides English-language interfaces.

Ride-Sharing Services: On-Demand Convenience

Ride-sharing services have gained popularity in Shenzhen, offering an on-demand alternative to taxis. Apps like Didi Chuxing allow users to request rides, view estimated fares, and pay digitally. These services provide a convenient and often cost-effective way to get around the city, with drivers familiar with navigation through their GPS systems.

Ride-sharing services can be particularly helpful for travelers who prefer English-language interfaces and cashless transactions.

Bicycles and E-Scooters: Green Commuting

For those who enjoy a more active mode of transportation, Shenzhen offers shared bicycles and electric scooters. These options promote eco-friendly commuting and allow riders to navigate shorter distances efficiently.

Shared bike services, like Ofo and Mobike, offer a convenient and inexpensive way to explore the city's neighborhoods and parks. Similarly, electric scooters, available for rent through various apps, provide a fun and agile means of getting around.

Considerations for Tourists:

- Transportation Card:Consider getting a transportation card (such as Shenzhen Tong) for seamless access to the metro, buses, and even some taxis. These cards offer convenience and can be recharged as needed.

- Apps: Download local transportation apps, such as the Shenzhen Metro app, Didi Chuxing, and bike-sharing apps, to navigate the city more efficiently.

- Language: While English signage and assistance are increasing, having some basic Chinese phrases or addresses written in Chinese characters can be helpful when communicating with drivers or seeking directions.

Shenzhen's diverse transportation options ensure that residents and visitors can choose the mode of travel that best suits their preferences and needs. Whether you're exploring the city's high-tech districts or its cultural enclaves, the transportation network ensures that you can traverse Shenzhen's vibrant landscape with ease.

Section 4: Accommodation

Hotel Options

Hong Kong offers a wide range of hotel options to cater to various preferences, from luxury accommodations with stunning views to budget-friendly options that provide comfort and convenience. Here are some of the best hotel choices across different categories in Hong Kong:

Luxury Hotels:

1. The Ritz-Carlton Hong Kong: This iconic hotel boasts breathtaking views from its harborfront location. With luxurious rooms, world-class dining, and a stunning rooftop bar, it's a favorite among luxury travelers.

2. Four Seasons Hotel Hong Kong: Situated in the heart of the city, this hotel offers impeccable service, elegant rooms, and a range of dining options. The rooftop pool and spa add to the luxurious experience.

3. Mandarin Oriental, Hong Kong: A true classic, this hotel offers a blend of luxury and sophistication. Its central location makes it convenient for both business and leisure travelers.

4. The Peninsula Hong Kong: Known for its historical charm and impeccable service, The Peninsula is an iconic hotel on the harborfront. Its afternoon tea is a must-try experience.

Mid-Range Hotels:

1. Hotel ICON: A design-forward hotel with modern amenities, Hotel ICON offers spacious rooms, a rooftop pool, and dining options that reflect Hong Kong's culinary diversity.

2. Ovolo Central: Located in the vibrant SoHo district, this stylish hotel offers chic rooms, a free minibar, and easy access to dining and nightlife.

3. Kerry Hotel, Hong Kong: Situated on the Kowloon waterfront, this contemporary hotel features spacious rooms, multiple dining options, and panoramic views of Victoria Harbour.

4. EAST, Hong Kong: With a focus on sustainability and modern design, EAST offers comfortable rooms, a rooftop bar, and a convenient location in Taikoo Shing.

Budget-Friendly Hotels:

1. iclub Sheung Wan Hotel: This hotel offers compact yet functional rooms at an affordable price. Its location in the trendy Sheung Wan neighborhood provides easy access to attractions.

2. Mini Hotel Central: With its modern and minimalist design, this budget-friendly option offers compact rooms in a central location, making it ideal for exploring the city.

3. Yesinn @Fortress Hill: A budget-friendly hostel option with clean and simple accommodations, Yesinn provides a convenient base for travelers looking to explore Hong Kong on a budget.

4. Homy Inn: Located in Tsim Sha Tsui, this budget hotel offers clean and comfortable rooms with a central location that's great for shopping and sightseeing.

Boutique Hotels:

1. Tuve: Known for its unique industrial-chic design, Tuve offers minimalist rooms and a tranquil atmosphere in the bustling Causeway Bay area.

2. The Jervois: This boutique hotel provides spacious and stylish suites with a modern design. It's situated in the vibrant Sheung Wan district.

3. Madera Hollywood: Offering quirky and artistic interiors, Madera Hollywood provides a unique boutique experience in the heart of SoHo.

Family-Friendly Hotels:

1. Disneyland Hotel: If you're traveling with family and planning to visit Hong Kong Disneyland, staying at the Disneyland Hotel offers a magical experience with themed rooms and convenient access to the park.

2. Regal Riverside Hotel: This hotel in Sha Tin provides family-friendly facilities, including a swimming pool and easy access to nearby attractions like the Ten Thousand Buddhas Monastery.

3. Cordis, Hong Kong: With spacious family rooms, a rooftop pool, and a kids' club, Cordis offers a comfortable and convenient stay for families.

Note: Prices and availability can vary based on the time of year, special events, and current circumstances. It's recommended to check the hotel's official website or reputable travel booking platforms for the most up-to-date information before making a reservation. Additionally, consider your preferred location, amenities, and budget when choosing the best hotel for your stay in Hong Kong.

The Ritz-Carlton Hong Kong: A Luxurious Haven of Elegance and Opulence

Perched high above the bustling cityscape of Hong Kong, The Ritz-Carlton Hong Kong stands as a pinnacle of luxury, offering an unparalleled experience that epitomizes elegance, opulence, and impeccable service. With its lofty location in the West Kowloon district, this iconic hotel has redefined hospitality, setting new standards for luxurious accommodations, gourmet dining, and breathtaking vistas that stretch to the horizon.

From the moment guests step into the grand lobby, they are enveloped in an ambiance of sophistication. The hotel's exquisite design seamlessly blends modern aesthetics with classic elements, creating a timeless atmosphere that pays homage to the city's rich history while embracing its forward-thinking spirit. Every detail, from the ornate chandeliers to the meticulously crafted furnishings, exudes an air of refinement that is a hallmark of The Ritz-Carlton brand.

Rooms and suites at The Ritz-Carlton Hong Kong are not merely accommodations; they are sanctuaries of comfort and indulgence. Each space is thoughtfully designed to provide an oasis of tranquility amidst the vibrant energy of Hong Kong. Floor-to-ceiling windows offer uninterrupted panoramic views of Victoria Harbour, the city skyline, and beyond, creating a breathtaking backdrop that seems to merge seamlessly with the luxurious interior.

The commitment to excellence extends to the dining experiences at The Ritz-Carlton Hong Kong, where culinary journeys are elevated to an art form. With several Michelin-starred restaurants under its roof, the hotel offers a gastronomic adventure that spans the globe. From the authentic Italian flavors of Tosca to the contemporary Cantonese cuisine at Tin Lung Heen, each restaurant is a testament to the mastery of the culinary arts.

One of the most captivating features of The Ritz-Carlton Hong Kong is undoubtedly Ozone, the highest bar in the world. Situated on the 118th floor, Ozone is more than just a bar—it's an elevation of the senses. As guests sip on expertly crafted cocktails, they are treated to panoramic views that stretch to the horizon, showcasing Hong Kong's skyline illuminated gainst the night sky. The experience is nothing short of breathtaking, offering a blend of luxury nd awe-inspiring beauty that is truly unforgettable.

or those seeking relaxation and rejuvenation, The Ritz-Carlton Spa is a sanctuary of wellness nd serenity. The spa's comprehensive range of treatments draws inspiration from both raditional Asian therapies and modern techniques, creating a holistic approach to well-being hat caters to the body, mind, and soul. The spa's tranquil ambiance, combined with the xpertise of skilled therapists, transports guests to a realm of blissful relaxation.

he Ritz-Carlton Hong Kong is more than a luxurious hotel; it's a destination in itself. The hotel's ky100 observation deck offers guests and visitors a chance to ascend to new heights and vitness the city from a vantage point that is both exhilarating and awe-inspiring. The nobstructed views from this iconic landmark provide a perspective of Hong Kong that is nparalleled, capturing the city's dynamism and energy in a single breathtaking panorama.

he dedication to providing unparalleled service is a hallmark of The Ritz-Carlton experience, nd The Ritz-Carlton Hong Kong is no exception. The hotel's staff members anticipate every eed, ensuring that each guest's stay is tailored to their desires. From personalized attention to iscreet assistance, the commitment to creating an unforgettable experience is evident in every nteraction.

n conclusion, The Ritz-Carlton Hong Kong stands as a testament to luxury, elegance, and the ursuit of perfection. From its lofty heights to its impeccable design, from its world-class dining o its unrivaled views, the hotel encapsulates the essence of sophistication that is synonymous vith The Ritz-Carlton brand. It is a destination that transcends mere accommodations, offering journey into a realm of refined indulgence and timeless beauty—a haven where guests can xperience the pinnacle of luxury that Hong Kong has to offer.

Four Seasons Hotel Hong Kong: Where Luxury and Panoramic Views Converge

lestled amid the vibrant cityscape of Hong Kong, the Four Seasons Hotel Hong Kong stands as n oasis of luxury, sophistication, and unparalleled service. With its prime location in the heart f the Central district, this iconic hotel redefines opulence and offers guests a world-class xperience that seamlessly blends Asian elegance with modern comforts.

rom the moment guests step into the elegant foyer, they are greeted by an ambiance of efined luxury that characterizes the Four Seasons brand. The hotel's interior design is a harmonious fusion of contemporary aesthetics and timeless Asian influences, creating an atmosphere that is both welcoming and awe-inspiring. Every detail, from the intricate artwork

to the sumptuous furnishings, exudes an air of sophistication that reflects Hong Kong's status a a global hub of culture and commerce.

Accommodations at the Four Seasons Hotel Hong Kong are a testament to comfort and indulgence. Each room and suite is a sanctuary of tranquility, offering a retreat from the city's hustle and bustle. Floor-to-ceiling windows showcase panoramic views of Victoria Harbour, the skyline, and the surrounding peaks, creating a mesmerizing backdrop that seamlessly complements the luxurious interior design.

Dining at the Four Seasons Hotel Hong Kong is a gastronomic journey that caters to the most discerning palates. The hotel is home to a collection of world-class restaurants, each offering a unique culinary experience. Caprice, a three-Michelin-star restaurant, presents an exquisite menu of French cuisine that celebrates flavors, textures, and artistry. Lung King Heen, the world's first Chinese restaurant to be awarded three Michelin stars, elevates Cantonese dining to new heights with its impeccable dishes and breathtaking views.

The Four Seasons Hotel Hong Kong takes relaxation and rejuvenation to new dimensions with Its state-of-the-art spa and wellness facilities. The award-winning Spa at Four Seasons offers a range of holistic treatments that combine traditional Asian techniques with modern therapies. Guests can indulge in luxurious massages, rejuvenating facials, and wellness programs that cater to both the body and soul. The spa's serene ambiance and skilled therapists provide an escape from the stresses of daily life, allowing guests to emerge revitalized and refreshed.

One of the hotel's most distinctive features is its infinity pool, which offers a surreal experience of swimming above the city's skyline. Perched on the hotel's rooftop, the pool provides an oasi of relaxation where guests can take a leisurely swim while gazing at the iconic skyline and Victoria Harbour. The rooftop also features a whirlpool and poolside lounges, creating a haven of tranquility amidst the urban landscape.

The Four Seasons Hotel Hong Kong seamlessly blends luxury with convenience, catering to the needs of both leisure and business travelers. The hotel's comprehensive business and event facilities offer a range of venues for meetings, conferences, and special occasions. With cutting-edge technology and personalized service, the hotel ensures that every event is executed flawlessly.

The commitment to unparalleled service is a hallmark of the Four Seasons experience, and the Four Seasons Hotel Hong Kong excels in this regard. The dedicated staff members go above and beyond to anticipate guests' needs, ensuring that every stay is personalized and memorable. From arranging exclusive experiences to providing discreet assistance, the hotel's attention to detail is evident in every interaction.

In conclusion, the Four Seasons Hotel Hong Kong is a masterpiece of luxury, sophistication, and panoramic views. From its stunning design to its world-class dining, from its wellness offerings

to its commitment to impeccable service, the hotel encapsulates the essence of opulence that defines the Four Seasons brand. It is a sanctuary of indulgence where guests can escape the ordinary and immerse themselves in a world of elegance and refinement—a haven that captures the essence of Hong Kong's allure and offers an unforgettable experience of the city's dynamic beauty.

Mandarin Oriental, Hong Kong: A Paradigm of Elegance and Timeless Luxury

Nestled in the heart of the bustling Central district, the Mandarin Oriental, Hong Kong stands as a beacon of sophistication, offering an extraordinary experience that seamlessly marries traditional elegance with modern comforts. With a legacy dating back to the 1960s, this iconic hotel has not only been a witness to Hong Kong's evolution but has also played a pivotal role in shaping the city's reputation as a global hub of luxury and refinement.

The moment guests step into the majestic foyer of the Mandarin Oriental, Hong Kong, they are transported to a realm of timeless luxury and unparalleled service. The hotel's interior exudes an air of understated opulence, with classic design elements, sumptuous furnishings, and exquisite artwork that pay homage to the city's rich heritage. Every corner exudes a sense of refined elegance that reflects the hotel's status as a haven of sophistication.

Accommodations at the Mandarin Oriental, Hong Kong are synonymous with indulgence and comfort. Each room and suite is a sanctuary of tranquility, meticulously designed to provide a sense of serenity amidst the bustling urban energy. The rooms are adorned with luxurious fabrics, elegant furnishings, and modern amenities that cater to the needs of both leisure and business travelers. Many of the rooms offer breathtaking views of Victoria Harbour, the city skyline, and the lush greenery that surrounds the hotel.

Dining at the Mandarin Oriental, Hong Kong is a gastronomic journey that tantalizes the senses. The hotel boasts an array of world-class restaurants that cater to diverse palates. Amber, a two-Michelin-star restaurant, presents contemporary French cuisine that showcases innovative flavors and artistic presentation. Man Wah, a celebrated Cantonese restaurant, offers traditional dishes in an opulent setting that captures the essence of Chinese culture. Each dining venue is a culinary masterpiece, embodying the hotel's commitment to exquisite gastronomy.

The Mandarin Oriental, Hong Kong's commitment to holistic well-being is evident in its spa and wellness facilities. The award-winning Mandarin Spa offers a haven of tranquility, where guests can indulge in rejuvenating treatments inspired by ancient Asian traditions. The spa's serene ambiance, skilled therapists, and range of therapies create an experience that is both restorative and revitalizing. The hotel also offers a state-of-the-art fitness center and a wellness program that caters to the body, mind, and spirit.

One of the hotel's most iconic features is its rooftop pool, which offers a sanctuary of relaxation amidst the city's dynamic energy. Surrounded by lush greenery and overlooking the breathtaking skyline, the pool provides a tranquil oasis where guests can escape the urban hustle and bask in the lap of luxury. The poolside lounges offer a space for guests to unwind and soak in the beauty of Hong Kong's iconic vistas.

The Mandarin Oriental, Hong Kong seamlessly blends luxury with convenience, catering to both leisure and business travelers. The hotel's extensive business and event facilities provide a range of venues for meetings, conferences, and special occasions. With advanced technology and personalized service, the hotel ensures that every event is executed flawlessly.

Service is at the core of the Mandarin Oriental experience, and the Mandarin Oriental, Hong Kong excels in this regard. The dedicated staff members epitomize the hotel's commitment to impeccable service, anticipating guests' needs and ensuring that every aspect of their stay is personalized. From arranging exclusive experiences to providing discreet assistance, the hotel's attention to detail is a testament to its unwavering dedication to guest satisfaction.

In conclusion, the Mandarin Oriental, Hong Kong is a testament to elegance, sophistication, and timeless luxury. With its rich history, opulent design, exquisite dining, and commitment to holistic well-being, the hotel encapsulates the essence of refined indulgence that defines the Mandarin Oriental brand. It is a destination where guests can immerse themselves in a world of unparalleled comfort and beauty—a haven that captures the essence of Hong Kong's allure and offers an unforgettable experience of the city's dynamic elegance.

The Peninsula Hong Kong: Where Heritage and Luxury Converge

Nestled along the bustling waterfront of Victoria Harbour, The Peninsula Hong Kong stands as an emblem of timeless luxury and refined heritage. With a legacy that spans nearly a century, this iconic hotel has played an instrumental role in shaping Hong Kong's reputation as a global hub of opulence, sophistication, and impeccable service.

Upon entering the grand foyer of The Peninsula Hong Kong, guests are transported into a world where history and modernity intertwine. The hotel's interior exudes an air of classic elegance, characterized by its colonial architecture, intricate details, and sumptuous furnishings. Every corner is a testament to the hotel's storied past, reflecting its role as a historic landmark that has borne witness to the city's evolution.

Accommodations at The Peninsula Hong Kong are synonymous with luxury and indulgence. Each room and suite is a sanctuary of tranquility, meticulously designed to provide a sense of respite amidst the urban energy. The rooms are adorned with luxurious fabrics, opulent décor, and modern amenities that cater to the needs of both leisure and business travelers. Many of the rooms offer sweeping views of Victoria Harbour, the city's skyline, and the iconic Star Ferry plying its route.

Dining at The Peninsula Hong Kong is a culinary journey that celebrates flavors, traditions, and innovation. The hotel boasts an array of dining venues that cater to diverse palates. Gaddi's, an acclaimed French restaurant, offers a lavish dining experience that pays homage to classic culinary techniques. Felix, with its avant-garde design, serves contemporary European cuisine against the backdrop of panoramic views. Each dining establishment is a testament to the hotel's commitment to gastronomic excellence.

The Peninsula Hong Kong's commitment to holistic well-being is manifested in its spa and wellness facilities. The Peninsula Spa offers a haven of rejuvenation, where guests can indulge in a range of treatments inspired by traditional Asian therapies. The spa's serene ambiance, skilled therapists, and personalized approach create an experience that is both revitalizing and transformative. The hotel's wellness program also includes a state-of-the-art fitness center, providing a comprehensive retreat for guests seeking to restore balance.

The Peninsula Hong Kong Is renowned for its iconic fleet of green Rolls-Royce limousines, a symbol of luxury and elegance that offers guests transportation in unparalleled style. The fleet provides a distinctive way to explore the city and its landmarks, encapsulating the hotel's commitment to providing unique and unforgettable experiences.

One of the hotel's most notable features is its legendary Afternoon Tea, a tradition that has been cherished for decades. Served in the elegant Lobby, the tea experience is a blend of culinary artistry, timeless rituals, and impeccable service. Guests are treated to an array of delectable treats, along with a selection of teas, creating an atmosphere of indulgence and refinement that is quintessentially Peninsula.

The Peninsula Hong Kong seamlessly marries tradition with modern luxury, catering to the needs of both contemporary travelers and those seeking to relive the glamour of a bygone era. The hotel's comprehensive business and event facilities offer a range of venues for meetings,

conferences, and special occasions. With cutting-edge technology and personalized service, the hotel ensures that every event is executed flawlessly.

Service is at the core of The Peninsula experience, and The Peninsula Hong Kong excels in this regard. The dedicated staff members epitomize the hotel's commitment to impeccable service, anticipating guests' needs and ensuring that every aspect of their stay is tailored to perfection. From arranging exclusive experiences to providing discreet assistance, the hotel's attention to detail is a testament to its unwavering dedication to guest satisfaction.

In conclusion, The Peninsula Hong Kong is a testament to heritage, luxury, and refined elegance. With its rich history, opulent design, culinary mastery, and commitment to holistic well-being, the hotel encapsulates the essence of a timeless haven that defines The Peninsula brand. It is a destination where guests can immerse themselves in a world of unparalleled opulence and sophistication—a sanctuary that captures the essence of Hong Kong's allure and offers an unforgettable experience of the city's dynamic charm.

MID-RANGE HOTELS

Hotel ICON: A Fusion of Innovation, Art, and Luxury

Nestled in the heart of the bustling Tsim Sha Tsui district, Hotel ICON stands as a testament to innovation, artistry, and luxury in the hospitality industry. With a mission to inspire, educate, and delight its guests, this iconic hotel has redefined the concept of modern accommodations, offering an immersive experience that seamlessly blends cutting-edge design with exceptional service.

From the moment guests step into the lobby of Hotel ICON, they are greeted by an environment that fuses contemporary aesthetics with artistic expressions. The hotel's interior design reflects a commitment to pushing boundaries, with bold architecture, vibrant colors, and creative installations that challenge the conventional norms of luxury hospitality. Every detail, from the avant-garde furnishings to the captivating artwork, contributes to an ambiance that is both inviting and thought-provoking.

Accommodations at Hotel ICON are a harmonious blend of comfort, style, and functionality. Each room and suite is thoughtfully designed to provide a haven of relaxation amidst the dynamic urban energy. The rooms are characterized by their modern furnishings, sleek lines,

and state-of-the-art technology that caters to the needs of contemporary travelers. The hotel's commitment to sustainability is evident in its eco-friendly initiatives and energy-efficient features that prioritize both guest comfort and environmental responsibility.

Dining at Hotel ICON is a culinary journey that celebrates flavors, creativity, and global influences. The hotel boasts an array of dining venues that cater to diverse palates. Above & Beyond, a Michelin-recommended Cantonese restaurant, offers an authentic experience that reflects the essence of Chinese cuisine. The Market, with its interactive open kitchen, showcases a variety of international dishes prepared with locally sourced ingredients. Each restaurant is a testament to the hotel's dedication to culinary excellence.

Hotel ICON places a strong emphasis on art and design, evident in its commitment to showcasing contemporary artwork throughout the property. The hotel's collaboration with the Hong Kong Polytechnic University's School of Hotel and Tourism Management has resulted in an innovative approach to integrating art and hospitality. The "Tomorrow's Guestrooms" initiative, which allows students to design guestrooms, offers a fresh perspective on modern living spaces and further establishes the hotel as a platform for creativity and innovation.

The hotel's dedication to holistic well-being is evident in its spa and wellness facilities. Angsana Spa offers a range of treatments that draw inspiration from traditional Asian therapies, providing guests with a sanctuary of relaxation and rejuvenation. The spa's tranquil ambiance, skilled therapists, and range of therapies create an experience that promotes both physical and mental well-being.

Hotel ICON's commitment to education extends beyond its partnership with the university. The hotel's unique "ICON 36" program provides an immersive learning experience for students interested in the hospitality industry. Students have the opportunity to gain hands-on experience and learn from industry professionals, enriching their knowledge and skills.

One of the hotel's distinctive features is its Above & Beyond Rooftop Lounge, which offers panoramic views of the city's skyline and Victoria Harbour. The lounge provides an ideal setting for guests to unwind, socialize, and enjoy creative cocktails and delectable snacks while taking in the breathtaking vistas.

In addition to its innovative approach to hospitality, Hotel ICON places great emphasis on sustainability and social responsibility. The hotel's commitment to reducing its environmental footprint is evident in its initiatives to minimize waste, conserve energy, and support local communities.

In conclusion, Hotel ICON is a fusion of innovation, art, and luxury that challenges traditional notions of hospitality. With its forward-thinking design, culinary excellence, dedication to well-being, and commitment to education, the hotel encapsulates the essence of a modern haven that is both inspiring and enriching. It is a destination where guests can immerse themselves in

a world of contemporary creativity and luxury—a platform that captures the essence of Hong Kong's evolving spirit and offers an unforgettable experience of the city's dynamic allure.

Ovolo Central: Where Trendsetting Design and Vibrant Energy Converge

Nestled in the heart of Hong Kong's vibrant SoHo district, Ovolo Central stands as a testament to trendsetting design, modern comfort, and an electrifying ambiance. With a commitment to providing a unique and unforgettable experience, this boutique hotel has redefined the concept of contemporary accommodations, offering a fusion of urban chic and personalized hospitality that resonates with the city's dynamic spirit.

Upon entering Ovolo Central, guests are welcomed into an environment that exudes an air of playful sophistication. The hotel's interior design showcases a fusion of bold colors, innovative materials, and quirky art installations, creating an atmosphere that is both inviting and stylish. Every detail, from the eclectic furnishings to the vibrant artwork, contributes to an ambiance that celebrates individuality and creativity.

Accommodations at Ovolo Central are a blend of comfort, style, and innovation. Each room and suite is thoughtfully designed to provide a comfortable retreat from the bustling urban energy. The rooms feature modern furnishings, vibrant décor, and amenities that cater to the needs of contemporary travelers. The hotel's commitment to sustainability is reflected in its eco-friendly initiatives, including energy-efficient features and the use of recycled materials.

Dining at Ovolo Central is a culinary adventure that embraces flavors, diversity, and a sense of community. The hotel boasts a range of dining venues that cater to different palates. Komune, the hotel's signature restaurant, offers a vibrant menu that reflects Hong Kong's multiculturalism, with dishes inspired by international cuisine. The restaurant's communal table encourages social interaction and provides a platform for guests to connect over shared experiences.

Ovolo Central places a strong emphasis on delivering a holistic guest experience through its "Loosey Goosey" philosophy. This approach aims to create a sense of freedom, where guests can truly be themselves and enjoy a stress-free stay. The hotel's commitment to personalized service and attention to detail is evident in its efforts to cater to individual preferences and create a welcoming environment that feels like a home away from home.

The hotel's dedication to well-being is reflected in its fitness facilities and wellness offerings. The well-equipped gym allows guests to maintain their fitness routines while traveling, and the hotel's central location provides easy access to outdoor activities and attractions that promote an active lifestyle.

One of the hotel's unique features is its inclusion of various complimentary amenities that enhance the guest experience. These amenities include a free minibar, in-room snacks, and even a daily "Social Hour" where guests can enjoy complimentary drinks and canapés in the communal lounge.

Ovolo Central's commitment to embracing technology is evident in its seamless integration of modern conveniences. The hotel offers guests high-speed Wi-Fi, smart TVs, and the use of a smartphone that allows for unlimited local and international calls. This tech-savvy approach caters to the needs of modern travelers who rely on connectivity and convenience.

In addition to its contemporary design and hospitality offerings, Ovolo Central is also a strong advocate for social responsibility. The hotel engages in various initiatives to give back to the community, support local causes, and promote sustainability.

In conclusion, Ovolo Central is a celebration of design, creativity, and a vibrant atmosphere. With its trendsetting interiors, community-driven approach, commitment to well-being, and dedication to social responsibility, the hotel encapsulates the essence of a modern boutique haven that resonates with Hong Kong's urban energy. It is a destination where guests can immerse themselves in a world of playful luxury and connect with the city's evolving spirit—a space that captures the essence of Hong Kong's dynamic charm and offers an unforgettable experience of its contemporary allure.

Kerry Hotel, Hong Kong: A Fusion of Modern Elegance and Urban Retreat

Nestled on the picturesque Kowloon waterfront, the Kerry Hotel, Hong Kong stands as an embodiment of modern elegance, contemporary design, and urban retreat. With a commitment to offering a seamless blend of comfort, style, and personalized service, this iconic hotel has redefined luxury accommodations, providing guests with a haven of relaxation that captures the dynamic spirit of the city.

From the moment guests step into the Kerry Hotel's expansive lobby, they are enveloped in an atmosphere of understated sophistication. The hotel's interior design seamlessly combines sleek

lines, natural elements, and stylish furnishings, creating an ambiance that is both inviting and chic. Every detail, from the open spaces to the carefully chosen artwork, contributes to an environment that reflects the hotel's dedication to modern aesthetics.

Accommodations at the Kerry Hotel, Hong Kong are a testament to contemporary comfort and urban luxury. Each room and suite is thoughtfully designed to offer a respite from the bustling cityscape, with panoramic views of Victoria Harbor or the surrounding landscape. The rooms feature modern amenities, plush furnishings, and an elegant color palette that creates a calming atmosphere for guests to unwind and rejuvenate.

Dining at the Kerry Hotel is a culinary journey that celebrates global flavors, innovation, and sustainability. The hotel offers a diverse range of dining options that cater to various palates. The Dockyard, an interactive food hall, provides a vibrant atmosphere where guests can explore a variety of international cuisines. Big Bay Café showcases an array of gourmet dishes prepared with locally sourced ingredients, emphasizing the hotel's commitment to supporting the community and offering a farm-to-table dining experience.

The Kerry Hotel, Hong Kong places a strong emphasis on holistic well-being, offering guests a sanctuary of relaxation and rejuvenation. The hotel's wellness facilities include a well-equipped fitness center and an infinity pool that overlooks Victoria Harbour. The hotel's serene ambiance and wellness program provide an opportunity for guests to prioritize their physical and mental well-being during their stay.

The hotel's dedication to personalized service is evident in its approach to creating memorable experiences for guests. The Kerry Concierge program offers curated itineraries and recommendations to help guests explore the city's hidden gems, ensuring that their stay is tailored to their preferences and interests.

One of the hotel's standout features is its outdoor landscaped terrace, which offers a unique oasis in the heart of the city. The terrace provides a tranquil setting where guests can relax, ocialize, and enjoy the panoramic views of the harbor and skyline. It's an ideal space for unwinding amidst the urban energy and taking in the breathtaking vistas.

Kerry Hotel, Hong Kong also values its role in promoting sustainability and social responsibility. The hotel's commitment to reducing its environmental impact is reflected in its eco-friendly initiatives and efforts to minimize waste and energy consumption.

In conclusion, the Kerry Hotel, Hong Kong is a testament to modern elegance, contemporary design, and urban tranquility. With its stylish interiors, diverse dining offerings, commitment to well-being, and dedication to personalized service, the hotel encapsulates the essence of a modern urban haven that resonates with the dynamic spirit of Hong Kong. It is a destination where guests can immerse themselves in a world of comfort and style—a retreat that captures

the essence of the city's allure and offers an unforgettable experience of its contemporary charm.

EAST, Hong Kong: A Fusion of Contemporary Design and Urban Sophistication

Nestled in the vibrant district of Quarry Bay, EAST, Hong Kong stands as a testament to contemporary design, urban sophistication, and a dynamic lifestyle. With a commitment to offering a unique and refreshing hospitality experience, this modern hotel has redefined the concept of urban accommodations, providing guests with a seamless blend of comfort, style, and personalized service that mirrors the city's progressive spirit.

The moment guests enter EAST, Hong Kong, they are greeted by an ambiance that radiates a sense of modernity and urban cool. The hotel's interior design showcases clean lines, minimalist aesthetics, and functional elegance that reflect the city's dynamic pace. Every aspect of the design, from the sleek furnishings to the innovative use of space, contributes to an atmosphere that celebrates contemporary living.

Accommodations at EAST, Hong Kong exemplify comfort and style. Each room and suite is thoughtfully designed to provide a haven of relaxation amidst the bustling city. The rooms feature modern amenities, streamlined décor, and an abundance of natural light, creating an inviting environment for guests to unwind and rejuvenate. The hotel's commitment to sustainability is evident in its eco-friendly initiatives, which include energy-efficient features and environmentally conscious practices.

Dining at EAST, Hong Kong is a gastronomic journey that emphasizes fresh ingredients, innovative flavors, and a modern culinary approach. The hotel offers a range of dining options that cater to diverse palates. Feast, the hotel's all-day dining restaurant, presents an array of international cuisines in a contemporary setting. Sugar, the rooftop bar, offers panoramic views of Victoria Harbor and the city skyline, providing a chic backdrop for sipping cocktails and socializing.

EAST, Hong Kong places a strong emphasis on creating a holistic guest experience that embraces well-being and urban exploration. The hotel's well-equipped fitness center allows guests to maintain their wellness routines while traveling. The hotel's central location provides easy access to the city's attractions, parks, and waterfront promenades, promoting an active lifestyle and encouraging guests to explore their surroundings.

The hotel's dedication to personalized service Is evident in its approach to guest engagement. The EAST experience is tailored to cater to the unique preferences and needs of each individual ensuring that every stay is memorable and meaningful. The hotel's Guest Experience Team is always on hand to provide recommendations and assistance, enabling guests to discover the hidden gems of Hong Kong.

EAST, Hong Kong places an emphasis on innovation and technology, evident in its seamless integration of modern conveniences. The hotel offers guests high-speed Wi-Fi, smart TVs, and a mobile app that allows for easy access to various hotel services. This tech-forward approach caters to the needs of modern travelers who seek connectivity and convenience at their fingertips.

In addition to its commitment to contemporary design and hospitality, EAST, Hong Kong values sustainability and social responsibility. The hotel is dedicated to minimizing its environmental impact and actively participates in initiatives that benefit the local community.

In conclusion, EAST, Hong Kong is a celebration of contemporary design, urban living, and personalized service. With its sleek interiors, diverse dining options, commitment to well-being, and dedication to sustainability, the hotel encapsulates the essence of a modern lifestyle haven that resonates with the city's dynamic spirit. It is a destination where guests can immerse themselves in a world of style and comfort—a retreat that captures the essence of Hong Kong's urban allure and offers an unforgettable experience of its contemporary charm.

BUDGET-FRIENDLY HOTELS

iclub Sheung Wan Hotel: A Modern Haven in the Heart of Hong Kong

Nestled in the vibrant district of Sheung Wan, iclub Sheung Wan Hotel stands as a contemporary haven that combines sleek design, urban convenience, and affordable luxury. With a commitment to offering a seamless blend of comfort, efficiency, and personalized service, this modern hotel has redefined the concept of urban accommodations, providing guests with a sanctuary of relaxation and convenience that reflects the city's dynamic energy.

From the moment guests step into the chic lobby of iclub Sheung Wan Hotel, they are greeted by an ambiance that exudes a sense of modernity and practicality. The hotel's interior design showcases clean lines, functional aesthetics, and a minimalist approach that resonates with the city's fast-paced lifestyle. Every aspect of the design, from the efficient use of space to the contemporary furnishings, contributes to an atmosphere that embraces the essence of modern urban living.

Accommodations at iclub Sheung Wan Hotel epitomize efficiency and comfort. Each room is thoughtfully designed to provide a cozy retreat from the city's hustle and bustle. The rooms feature modern amenities, smart storage solutions, and a soothing color palette that creates a relaxing environment for guests to unwind and recharge. The hotel's commitment to sustainability is evident in its eco-friendly initiatives, which include energy-efficient features and environmentally conscious practices.

Dining at iclub Sheung Wan Hotel is a straightforward and convenient experience that caters to the needs of busy travelers. The hotel offers a grab-and-go café that provides a selection of light snacks, beverages, and breakfast options. This practical approach allows guests to enjoy quick and delicious bites as they navigate their itinerary or head out for a day of exploration.

iclub Sheung Wan Hotel places a strong emphasis on efficiency and convenience, aligning with the needs of modern travelers. The hotel offers a self-service laundry room, allowing guests to easily refresh their wardrobes during their stay. The hotel's central location provides easy access to public transportation, attractions, and business districts, making it an ideal choice for both leisure and business travelers who seek a hassle-free experience.

The hotel's dedication to personalized service is evident in its commitment to guest comfort and convenience. The iclub Hotel app provides guests with a platform to access various hotel services, such as check-in and check-out, restaurant reservations, and information about local attractions. This digital approach streamlines the guest experience and offers a modern solution for staying connected with the hotel's offerings.

Iclub Sheung Wan Hotel embraces technology as a means of enhancing guest convenience. The hotel offers high-speed Wi-Fi and smart TVs in each room, catering to the needs of tech-savvy travelers who seek connectivity and entertainment options during their stay.

In addition to its contemporary design and practical hospitality offerings, iclub Sheung Wan Hotel values sustainability and social responsibility. The hotel is dedicated to minimizing its environmental impact and actively engages in initiatives that contribute positively to the local community.

In conclusion, iclub Sheung Wan Hotel is a celebration of modern efficiency, urban living, and practical luxury. With its functional interiors, convenient dining options, commitment to sustainability, and dedication to personalized service, the hotel encapsulates the essence of a

modern lifestyle haven that resonates with the city's dynamic spirit. It is a destination where guests can immerse themselves in a world of convenience and comfort—a retreat that capture the essence of Hong Kong's urban allure and offers an unforgettable experience of its contemporary charm.

Mini Hotel Central: Affordable Comfort in the Heart of Hong Kong

Nestled in the bustling Central district, Mini Hotel Central offers a unique blend of affordability, convenience, and comfort for travelers seeking a budget-friendly option in the heart of Hong Kong. With a commitment to providing a no-frills yet stylish accommodation experience, this compact hotel has redefined the concept of affordable urban stays, offering guests a simple and efficient base to explore the city's dynamic offerings.

From the moment guests step into Mini Hotel Central's compact yet chic lobby, they are greeted by an ambiance that embodies modern simplicity. The hotel's interior design features minimalist aesthetics, functional furnishings, and a straightforward layout that resonates with the practical needs of budget-conscious travelers. Every element of the design, from the efficient use of space to the contemporary décor, contributes to an atmosphere that caters to those who value value and convenience.

Accommodations at Mini Hotel Central are designed to maximize space without compromising on comfort. Each room is thoughtfully laid out to offer a cozy and efficient place to rest after a ay of exploring the city. The rooms feature modern amenities, smart storage solutions, and a lean design that creates a relaxing environment for guests to unwind and recharge. The hotel's commitment to sustainability is reflected in its eco-friendly initiatives, which include energy-fficient features and environmentally conscious practices.

Dining at Mini Hotel Central is catered to those who appreciate simplicity and convenience. The otel offers a communal kitchenette, where guests can prepare their own meals or enjoy a uick snack. This self-service option adds an element of practicality to the stay, allowing guests o save on dining expenses while also fostering a sense of community.

Mini Hotel Central places a strong emphasis on efficiency and accessibility, aligned with the eeds of travelers who are constantly on the go. The hotel's location in the heart of Central rovides easy access to public transportation, shopping districts, and cultural attractions, naking it an ideal choice for those who want to make the most of their time in the city.

he hotel's dedication to streamlined service is evident in its commitment to self-check-in and igital solutions. The hotel's online platform allows guests to manage their bookings, check in nd out, and access information about local attractions with ease. This approach minimizes nnecessary interactions and adds a layer of convenience for guests who prefer a self-directed xperience.

Mini Hotel Central embraces technology to enhance the guest experience. The hotel provides igh-speed Wi-Fi, smart TVs, and other tech amenities that cater to the needs of modern ravelers who seek connectivity and entertainment options during their stay.

n addition to its focus on affordability and practicality, Mini Hotel Central values sustainability nd responsible hospitality. The hotel is dedicated to minimizing its environmental impact and ctively participates in initiatives that contribute positively to the local community.

n conclusion, Mini Hotel Central is a celebration of affordable comfort, practical living, and nodern efficiency. With its no-frills interiors, self-service dining options, commitment to ustainability, and dedication to streamlined service, the hotel encapsulates the essence of an ffordable urban haven that caters to the needs of budget-conscious travelers. It is a estination where guests can immerse themselves in a world of convenience and simplicity—a etreat that captures the essence of Hong Kong's dynamic allure and offers an unforgettable xperience of practical urban living.

Yesinn @Fortress Hill: A Budget-Friendly Oasis in Vibrant Hong Kong

Nestled in the bustling district of Fortress Hill, Yesinn @Fortress Hill offers budget-conscious travelers a comfortable and convenient oasis in the heart of Hong Kong. With a commitment to providing affordable yet cozy accommodations, this budget hostel has redefined the concept of budget travel, offering guests a simple and practical base from which to explore the city's diverse offerings.

From the moment travelers step into Yesinn @Fortress Hill's welcoming reception area, they are greeted by an environment that embodies functional simplicity. The hostel's interior design features practical furnishings, efficient layout, and a straightforward approach that caters to travelers seeking affordable comfort without unnecessary frills. Every aspect of the design, from the communal spaces to the cozy dormitories, contributes to an atmosphere that fosters a sense of community and shared experiences.

Accommodations at Yesinn @Fortress Hill are designed to maximize comfort within a budget-friendly framework. The hostel offers dormitory-style rooms that provide a cost-effective option for travelers looking to connect with fellow adventurers. The rooms are equipped with modern amenities, secure lockers, and essential comforts that create a cozy environment for guests to rest and recharge. The hostel's commitment to sustainability is reflected in its eco-friendly practices, including energy-efficient features and efforts to reduce waste.

Yesinn @Fortress Hill understands the needs of budget travelers who prioritize efficient and convenient dining options. The hostel offers a communal kitchenette, where guests can prepare their own meals and snacks. This self-service option adds practicality to the stay, allowing travelers to save on dining expenses while also fostering a sense of camaraderie among fellow guests.

The hostel's strategic location in Fortress Hill offers guests easy access to public transportation, shopping districts, and cultural attractions, making it an ideal choice for those who want to explore the city without breaking the bank. The hostel's central location ensures that travelers can make the most of their time in Hong Kong, whether they're interested in sightseeing, shopping, or indulging in local cuisine.

Yesinn @Fortress Hill embraces a community-driven approach to hospitality, providing guests with opportunities to connect with fellow travelers and share their experiences. The hostel's communal spaces, including the lounge and common areas, offer a platform for socializing, swapping travel stories, and forming new friendships. This communal atmosphere adds a sense of warmth and camaraderie that resonates with backpackers and budget travelers.

The hostel's commitment to providing a seamless experience for guests is evident in its approach to efficient service. The hostel's staff members are friendly and knowledgeable, offering assistance and recommendations to help guests make the most of their stay. Additionally, the hostel's online platform allows travelers to manage their bookings, check-in, and access information about local attractions with ease.

Yesinn @Fortress Hill understands the importance of connectivity for modern travelers. The hostel offers complimentary high-speed Wi-Fi and other tech amenities that cater to the needs of travelers who seek connectivity and digital convenience during their stay.

In addition to its focus on affordability, Yesinn @Fortress Hill values sustainability and responsible hospitality. The hostel actively engages in initiatives that contribute positively to the local community and environment.

In conclusion, Yesinn @Fortress Hill is a celebration of budget-friendly comfort, communal living, and practicality. With its functional interiors, self-service amenities, commitment to sustainability, and dedication to fostering connections among travelers, the hostel encapsulates the essence of affordable travel that resonates with the spirit of exploration. It is a destination

where guests can immerse themselves in a world of shared experiences and affordability—a retreat that captures the essence of Hong Kong's dynamic allure and offers an unforgettable experience of budget travel in a vibrant urban setting.

Homy Inn: A Cozy Retreat in the Heart of Hong Kong

Nestled in the vibrant cityscape of Tsim Sha Tsui, Homy Inn offers travelers a warm and welcoming haven that combines comfort, affordability, and convenience. With a commitment to providing a home away from home, this boutique guesthouse has redefined the concept of cozy accommodations, offering guests a personal and intimate experience that mirrors the city's dynamic charm.

From the moment guests step into Homy Inn's charming lobby, they are embraced by an ambiance that exudes comfort and intimacy. The guesthouse's interior design features a blend of modern aesthetics and a homely atmosphere, creating an environment that fosters a sense of relaxation and familiarity. Every aspect of the design, from the warm color palette to the carefully selected furnishings, contributes to an atmosphere that resonates with those seeking a personalized stay.

Accommodations at Homy Inn are designed to provide a comfortable retreat after a day of exploration in the bustling city. The guesthouse offers a variety of room types to cater to different traveler preferences, from solo adventurers to families. The rooms feature essential amenities, cozy décor, and a welcoming ambiance that allows guests to unwind and recharge in a space that feels like their own.

Homy Inn understands the importance of efficient and convenient dining options for travelers on the go. The guesthouse offers a communal kitchenette, where guests can prepare simple meals and snacks at their convenience. This self-service option adds a layer of practicality to the stay, enabling travelers to enjoy their own culinary creations and experience a sense of home.

The guesthouse's strategic location in Tsim Sha Tsui offers guests easy access to the city's attractions, shopping districts, and cultural hotspots. Its proximity to public transportation hubs ensures that travelers can explore the city with ease, making the most of their time in Hong Kong. The guesthouse's central location allows guests to immerse themselves in the vibrant urban energy while having a cozy retreat to return to at the end of the day.

Homy Inn values personalized service and genuine hospitality, providing guests with a welcoming and attentive experience. The guesthouse's staff members are dedicated to ensuring that guests feel at ease and have all they need for a comfortable stay. Their local expertise and

willingness to assist with recommendations and information contribute to a sense of being taken care of during the stay.

Homy Inn offers a platform for travelers to connect and share their experiences. The communal lounge and common areas provide opportunities for guests to interact, exchange travel stories, and forge new friendships. This sense of camaraderie adds an extra layer of warmth and community that resonates with travelers seeking a social and inclusive atmosphere.

In addition to its focus on comfort and affordability, Homy Inn values sustainability and responsible hospitality. The guesthouse engages in initiatives that contribute positively to the local community and environment, aligning with its commitment to being a responsible and conscientious host.

In conclusion, Homy Inn is a celebration of coziness, personalized living, and genuine hospitality. With its warm interiors, communal spaces, commitment to sustainability, and dedication to creating a welcoming atmosphere, the guesthouse encapsulates the essence of a home away from home that resonates with the spirit of comfort and connection. It is a destination where guests can immerse themselves in a world of intimacy and relaxation—a retreat that captures the essence of Hong Kong's allure and offers an unforgettable experience of a cozy urban escape.

BOUTIQUE HOTELS

Tuve: A Minimalist Sanctuary in the Heart of Hong Kong

Nestled in the vibrant district of Tin Hau, Tuve offers travelers a unique and captivating haven that embodies minimalist design, tranquility, and modern luxury. With a commitment to providing a distinctive and immersive experience, this boutique hotel has redefined the concept of contemporary accommodations, offering guests a serene escape that resonates with the city's dynamic energy.

From the moment guests step into Tuve's serene lobby, they are enveloped by an ambiance that exudes simplicity and elegance. The hotel's interior design showcases a blend of clean lines, muted colors, and carefully curated furnishings, creating an atmosphere that fosters a sense of

calm and contemplation. Every detail, from the artistic installations to the subtle lighting, contributes to an environment that reflects the hotel's dedication to minimalist aesthetics.

Accommodations at Tuve epitomize modern luxury and tranquility. Each room and suite is thoughtfully designed to provide a peaceful retreat amidst the urban energy. The rooms feature a seamless integration of form and function, with sleek amenities, comfortable furnishings, and a neutral color palette that creates an environment conducive to relaxation and introspection. The hotel's commitment to sustainability is reflected in its eco-friendly practices and efforts to minimize waste.

Tuve places a strong emphasis on providing a tranquil escape from the bustling city, embracing the principles of mindfulness and serenity. The hotel's serene ambiance and minimalist approach create a space where guests can disconnect from the outside world and engage in moments of self-discovery and rejuvenation.

Dining at Tuve is an understated and refined experience that emphasizes quality and authenticity. The hotel offers a carefully curated selection of dining options that celebrate local flavors and international influences. The focus on quality ingredients and culinary craftsmanship ensures that each meal is a delightful exploration of tastes and textures.

The hotel's strategic location in Tin Hau offers guests a balance between urban exploration and retreat. Tuve's proximity to public transportation allows travelers to easily access the city's attractions and entertainment districts, while its serene environment provides a respite from the fast-paced cityscape.

Tuve's commitment to personalized service is evident in its approach to guest comfort and well being. The hotel's attentive staff members are dedicated to creating a seamless and memorable experience for every guest, from providing local recommendations to ensuring that individual needs are met with care and attention.

One of the hotel's standout features is its focus on art and aesthetics. Tuve collaborates with local artists and designers, showcasing unique installations and design elements throughout the property. This commitment to artistic expression adds a layer of depth and cultural enrichment to the guest experience.

In addition to its minimalist design and personalized service, Tuve values sustainability and responsible hospitality. The hotel actively engages in initiatives that contribute positively to the local community and environment, aligning with its commitment to ethical practices.

In conclusion, Tuve is a celebration of minimalist design, tranquility, and modern luxury. With its serene interiors, refined dining offerings, commitment to well-being, and dedication to artistic expression, the hotel encapsulates the essence of a contemporary haven that resonates with the city's dynamic spirit. It is a destination where guests can immerse themselves in a world of

beauty and mindfulness—a retreat that captures the essence of Hong Kong's allure and offers an unforgettable experience of modern sophistication in a tranquil urban setting.

The Jervois: Where Urban Sophistication Meets Contemporary Comfort

Nestled in the heart of Sheung Wan, The Jervois stands as a testament to urban sophistication, contemporary design, and personalized luxury. With a commitment to providing a refined and tailored experience, this boutique hotel has redefined the concept of modern accommodations, offering guests a haven of comfort and style that resonates with the city's dynamic allure.

From the moment guests step into The Jervois' elegant lobby, they are greeted by an ambiance that exudes timeless elegance and modern refinement. The hotel's interior design seamlessly combines sleek lines, luxurious materials, and stylish furnishings, creating an atmosphere that is both inviting and chic. Every detail, from the meticulously curated artwork to the thoughtfully designed common spaces, contributes to an environment that reflects the hotel's dedication to creating a space of understated luxury.

Accommodations at The Jervois epitomize modern comfort and tailored luxury. Each room and suite is meticulously designed to offer a spacious and sophisticated sanctuary within the urban landscape. The rooms feature high-end amenities, plush furnishings, and a color palette that creates a calming environment for guests to unwind and rejuvenate. The hotel's commitment to sustainability is evident in its eco-friendly initiatives and efforts to create a luxurious yet environmentally conscious space.

The Jervois offers an exceptional dining experience that celebrates culinary craftsmanship and quality ingredients. The hotel's dining options showcase a fusion of international flavors and local influences, resulting in a menu that caters to diverse palates. The emphasis on gastronomic excellence ensures that each meal is a delightful journey of flavors and textures, showcasing the hotel's dedication to creating an elevated dining experience for its guests.

The hotel's central location In Sheung Wan places guests at the crossroads of urban exploration and cultural immersion. The Jervois is ideally situated to offer easy access to Hong Kong's attractions, shopping districts, and entertainment hubs, making it a perfect choice for travelers who wish to experience the city's dynamic offerings while having a luxurious and comfortable retreat to return to.

The Jervois places a strong emphasis on personalized service and attention to detail. The hotel's dedicated staff members are committed to providing a seamless and tailored experience for each guest, from arranging bespoke experiences to ensuring that individual preferences are met with care and precision.

The hotel's commitment to well-being is reflected in its wellness offerings and fitness facilities. The Jervois provides guests with the opportunity to prioritize their physical and mental health during their stay, with access to a well-equipped gym and wellness programs that cater to their needs.

One of The Jervois' distinctive features is its focus on creating a home-like environment for guests. The hotel offers a range of serviced apartments that provide an extended-stay option for travelers seeking a luxurious and comfortable home away from home. These apartments are designed to provide all the comforts of a residence while offering the services and amenities of a luxury hotel.

In addition to its emphasis on luxury and personalized service, The Jervois values its role in promoting cultural enrichment and artistic expression. The hotel often collaborates with local artists and designers, showcasing unique art installations and design elements throughout the property. This commitment to creativity adds a layer of depth and cultural immersion to the guest experience.

In conclusion, The Jervois is a celebration of urban sophistication, modern luxury, and personalized comfort. With its elegant interiors, exceptional dining offerings, commitment to well-being, and dedication to artistic collaboration, the hotel encapsulates the essence of a refined urban haven that resonates with the city's dynamic spirit. It is a destination where guests can immerse themselves in a world of luxury and style—a retreat that captures the essence of Hong Kong's allure and offers an unforgettable experience of contemporary elegance in the heart of the city.

Madera Hollywood: Where Artistry and Comfort Converge

Nestled in the heart of the vibrant district of Sheung Wan, Madera Hollywood stands as a testament to artistic flair, contemporary design, and unparalleled comfort. With a commitment to offering a unique and immersive experience, this boutique hotel has redefined the concept of modern accommodations, providing guests with a haven that resonates with the city's dynamic energy and artistic spirit.

The moment guests step Into Madera Hollywood's artistic lobby, they are greeted by an ambiance that exudes creativity and innovation. The hotel's interior design seamlessly blends artistry, modern aesthetics, and luxurious comfort, creating an atmosphere that is both captivating and welcoming. Every detail, from the carefully curated artworks to the thoughtfully designed spaces, contributes to an environment that reflects the hotel's dedication to creating an immersive and inspiring atmosphere.

Accommodations at Madera Hollywood epitomize artistic elegance and contemporary comfort. Each room and suite is designed to provide a stylish and cozy sanctuary within the bustling city. The rooms feature high-end amenities, chic furnishings, and a color palette that creates a soothing environment for guests to unwind and recharge. The hotel's commitment to sustainability is evident in its eco-friendly initiatives and efforts to provide a luxurious yet environmentally conscious experience.

Madera Hollywood offers a culinary journey that celebrates flavors and ingredients from around the world. The hotel's dining options showcase a fusion of global influences and local culinary traditions, resulting in a menu that caters to diverse tastes. The emphasis on gastronomic excellence ensures that each meal is an exploration of tastes and textures, reflecting the hotel's dedication to creating an elevated dining experience for its guests.

The hotel's central location In Sheung Wan places guests at the crossroads of urban exploration and cultural immersion. Madera Hollywood is ideally situated to offer easy access to Hong Kong's attractions, shopping districts, and entertainment hubs, making it an ideal choice for travelers who wish to experience the city's dynamic offerings while having a luxurious and stylish retreat to return to.

Madera Hollywood places a strong emphasis on personalized service and guest well-being. The hotel's attentive staff members are committed to providing a seamless and memorable experience for each guest, from arranging bespoke experiences to ensuring that individual preferences are met with care and precision.

The hotel's commitment to artistic expression is reflected in its collaboration with local artists and designers. Madera Hollywood often showcases unique art installations and design elements throughout the property, creating a dynamic and inspiring environment that adds a layer of cultural enrichment to the guest experience.

One of Madera Hollywood's standout features is its rooftop bar and lounge, offering panoramic views of the city's skyline. This unique space provides an opportunity for guests to unwind, socialize, and enjoy breathtaking vistas while sipping on crafted cocktails or indulging in delectable bites.

In addition to its emphasis on artistry and personalized service, Madera Hollywood values its role in promoting sustainability and responsible hospitality. The hotel actively engages in

initiatives that contribute positively to the local community and environment, aligning with its commitment to ethical practices.

In conclusion, Madera Hollywood is a celebration of artistry, contemporary design, and immersive comfort. With its creative interiors, exceptional dining offerings, commitment to well-being, and dedication to artistic collaboration, the hotel encapsulates the essence of a modern urban haven that resonates with the city's dynamic spirit. It is a destination where guests can immerse themselves in a world of creativity and style—a retreat that captures the essence of Hong Kong's allure and offers an unforgettable experience of modern elegance and artistic inspiration.

FAMILY-FRIENDLY HOTELS:

Disneyland Hotel: Where Magic and Luxury Combine

Nestled in the enchanting world of Hong Kong Disneyland Resort, the Disneyland Hotel stands as a beacon of magic, wonder, and luxury. With a commitment to providing guests with an immersive and enchanting experience, this iconic hotel has redefined the concept of fairy-tale accommodations, offering families and Disney enthusiasts a dreamlike escape that captures the essence of imagination and joy.

From the moment guests step into the grand lobby of Disneyland Hotel, they are transported into a world of fantasy and enchantment. The hotel's architecture, inspired by Victorian elegance and Disney charm, creates an atmosphere that exudes classic storytelling and contemporary comfort. Every detail, from the intricate decorations to the whimsical touches, contributes to an environment that reflects the hotel's dedication to creating a space where dreams come to life.

Accommodations at Disneyland Hotel epitomize luxury and magical living. Each room and suite is designed to provide a regal retreat within the enchanting realm. The rooms feature high-end amenities, lavish furnishings, and touches of Disney magic that create a captivating environment for guests to unwind and relive their favorite fairy-tale moments. The hotel's commitment to guest comfort is evident in every aspect of the room design, from the plush bedding to the attention to detail that transports guests to a realm of fantasy.

Dining at Disneyland Hotel is an experience that caters to the young and young-at-heart. The hotel's dining options offer a variety of cuisines and culinary experiences that celebrate the magic of Disney characters and stories. From character breakfasts to themed afternoon teas, every meal is a delightful journey that allows guests to dine in the company of beloved Disney friends.

The hotel's location within Hong Kong Disneyland Resort offers guests an unparalleled opportunity to experience the magic of Disney. Being just moments away from the theme park's attractions, shows, and entertainment, Disneyland Hotel ensures that guests have easy access to a world of fantasy and adventure. The hotel's proximity to the park allows families and Disney enthusiasts to maximize their time exploring the enchanting offerings of the resort.

Disneyland Hotel places a strong emphasis on creating lasting memories for families and guests. The hotel's dedication to exceptional service ensures that every stay is personalized and tailored to the needs of each guest. From arranging special surprises to offering

ecommendations for an unforgettable Disney experience, the hotel's staff members are
:ommitted to adding a touch of magic to every moment.

)ne of the hotel's standout features is its lush gardens and outdoor spaces that evoke the
 :harm of a fairy-tale kingdom. These meticulously landscaped areas offer guests a serene and
•icturesque backdrop for relaxation, exploration, and play.

n addition to its emphasis on luxury and enchantment, Disneyland Hotel values its role in
:reating magical moments for guests of all ages. The hotel actively participates in initiatives that
•romote community engagement and responsible tourism, aligning with its commitment to
naking a positive impact.

n conclusion, Disneyland Hotel is a celebration of magic, luxury, and immersive living. With its
•nchanting interiors, exceptional dining experiences, commitment to guest comfort, and
ledication to creating Disney moments, the hotel encapsulates the essence of a fairy-tale
iaven that resonates with the spirit of imagination and joy. It is a destination where guests of
ill ages can immerse themselves in a world of fantasy and wonder—a retreat that captures the
•ssence of the Disney spirit and offers an unforgettable experience of enchantment and
lelight.

Regal Riverside Hotel: A Tranquil Oasis of Comfort and Elegance

Jestled on the banks of the picturesque Shing Mun River, the Regal Riverside Hotel stands as a
iaven of comfort, elegance, and serenity in the bustling city of Hong Kong. With a commitment
:o providing guests with a relaxing and rejuvenating experience, this well-established hotel has
edefined the concept of urban accommodations, offering a peaceful retreat that embraces
•oth modernity and natural beauty.

rom the moment guests step into the Regal Riverside Hotel's expansive lobby, they are
:reeted by an ambiance that exudes warmth and sophistication. The hotel's interior design
eamlessly combines classic aesthetics, modern elements, and natural materials, creating an

atmosphere that is both inviting and elegant. Every detail, from the soothing color palette to the tasteful furnishings, contributes to an environment that reflects the hotel's dedication to providing a space of comfort and refinement.

Accommodations at Regal Riverside Hotel epitomize modern comfort and serene living. Each room and suite is thoughtfully designed to offer a tranquil sanctuary amidst the city's hustle and bustle. The rooms feature contemporary amenities, plush furnishings, and a neutral color scheme that creates a calming environment for guests to unwind and recharge. The hotel's commitment to guest satisfaction is evident in its attention to detail and dedication to providing a comfortable and inviting space.

Dining at Regal Riverside Hotel is a culinary journey that celebrates global flavors and culinary excellence. The hotel's dining options offer a diverse range of cuisines and culinary experiences that cater to various tastes and preferences. From international buffets to specialty restaurants every meal is an opportunity for guests to indulge in delectable flavors and create memorable dining moments.

The hotel's location in the Sha Tin district offers guests a unique blend of urban convenience and natural tranquility. Regal Riverside Hotel is ideally situated to offer easy access to Hong Kong's attractions, shopping districts, and entertainment hubs, while also providing a serene and scenic environment away from the city's hustle. The hotel's setting on the riverbank adds an element of peacefulness that sets it apart from other urban accommodations.

Regal Riverside Hotel places a strong emphasis on providing a holistic experience for guests. The hotel's wellness facilities, including a fitness center and a swimming pool, allow guests to prioritize their physical and mental well-being during their stay. Additionally, the hotel offers spa

treatments and relaxation amenities that add an extra layer of rejuvenation to the guest experience.

The hotel's commitment to personalized service Is evident in its attentive staff members who are dedicated to creating a seamless and memorable experience for each guest. The hotel's team is always ready to assist with recommendations, arrangements, and ensuring that guests have all they need for a comfortable stay.

One of the hotel's standout features is its lush outdoor spaces that provide a serene and picturesque backdrop for relaxation and leisure. The beautifully landscaped gardens and riverfront promenade offer guests an opportunity to escape the urban environment and connect with nature.

In addition to its focus on guest comfort and elegance, Regal Riverside Hotel values sustainability and responsible hospitality. The hotel actively engages in initiatives that contribute positively to the local community and environment, aligning with its commitment to ethical practices.

In conclusion, Regal Riverside Hotel is a celebration of comfort, elegance, and natural beauty. With its inviting interiors, exceptional dining offerings, commitment to guest well-being, and dedication to creating a serene retreat, the hotel encapsulates the essence of a tranquil urban oasis that resonates with the city's dynamic spirit. It is a destination where guests can immerse themselves in a world of relaxation and refinement—a retreat that captures the essence of Hong Kong's allure and offers an unforgettable experience of comfort and serenity in a scenic and peaceful setting.

Cordis, Hong Kong: Where Luxury and Innovation Converge

Nestled in the heart of the bustling Mong Kok district, Cordis, Hong Kong stands as an embodiment of luxury, innovation, and exceptional service. With a commitment to providing guests with a transformative and immersive experience, this distinguished hotel has redefined the concept of urban accommodations, offering a haven of comfort and sophistication that resonates with the city's vibrant energy.

From the moment guests step into Cordis, Hong Kong's elegant lobby, they are enveloped by an ambiance that exudes elegance and modernity. The hotel's interior design seamlessly blends contemporary aesthetics, stylish furnishings, and cutting-edge technology, creating an

atmosphere that is both inviting and impressive. Every detail, from the captivating art installations to the sleek architectural elements, contributes to an environment that reflects the hotel's dedication to providing a space of luxurious living.

Accommodations at Cordis, Hong Kong epitomize modern comfort and refined living. Each room and suite is meticulously designed to offer a lavish retreat amidst the urban landscape. The rooms feature top-of-the-line amenities, plush furnishings, and an elegant color palette that creates an environment conducive to relaxation and indulgence. The hotel's commitment to guest satisfaction is evident in its meticulous attention to detail and the exceptional level of comfort provided in every room.

Dining at Cordis, Hong Kong is a gastronomic journey that celebrates culinary excellence and innovation. The hotel's dining options offer a diverse range of cuisines and gastronomic experiences that cater to various palates. From Michelin-starred dining to casual eateries, every culinary endeavor is an opportunity for guests to savor exceptional flavors and enjoy memorable dining moments.

The hotel's central location in Mong Kok offers guests a balance between urban exploration and cultural immersion. Cordis, Hong Kong is ideally situated to offer easy access to Hong Kong's attractions, shopping districts, and entertainment hubs, making it an ideal choice for travelers who wish to experience the city's dynamic offerings while having a luxurious and sophisticated retreat to return to.

Cordis, Hong Kong places a strong emphasis on personalized service and guest satisfaction. The hotel's attentive staff members are dedicated to providing an unparalleled and memorable experience for each guest, from arranging personalized services to ensuring that individual preferences are met with care and precision.

The hotel's commitment to innovation is reflected in its technological offerings and forward-thinking amenities. Cordis, Hong Kong provides guests with state-of-the-art technology that enhances the guest experience, from high-speed Wi-Fi to in-room smart controls. The hotel's dedication to staying at the forefront of innovation ensures that guests have access to the latest conveniences and comforts.

One of Cordis, Hong Kong's standout features is its commitment to wellness and holistic well-being. The hotel's wellness facilities, including a rooftop pool and a fully equipped fitness center, allow guests to prioritize their physical and mental health during their stay. Additionally, the hotel offers wellness programs, spa treatments, and relaxation amenities that add an extra layer of rejuvenation to the guest experience.

In addition to its emphasis on luxury and innovation, Cordis, Hong Kong values its role in creating positive social impact. The hotel actively engages in initiatives that contribute to the

local community, including sustainability programs and community outreach efforts, aligning with its commitment to making a difference.

In conclusion, Cordis, Hong Kong is a celebration of luxury, innovation, and exceptional living. With its modern interiors, exceptional dining offerings, commitment to guest satisfaction, and dedication to technological advancement, the hotel encapsulates the essence of sophisticated urban living that resonates with the city's dynamic spirit. It is a destination where guests can immerse themselves in a world of indulgence and modernity—a retreat that captures the essence of Hong Kong's allure and offers an unforgettable experience of opulence and elegance in the heart of the city.

Section 5: Exploring the Districts

Central and Sheung Wan: The Heartbeat of Hong Kong's Urban Charm

Nestled at the crossroads of tradition and modernity, Central and Sheung Wan stand as vibrant neighborhoods that pulse with the energy of Hong Kong's dynamic cityscape. These two adjoining districts offer a captivating blend of history, culture, commerce, and leisure, creating a rich tapestry of experiences that reflect the city's unique character. From towering skyscrapers to quaint alleys, bustling markets to high-end boutiques, Central and Sheung Wan encapsulate the essence of Hong Kong's urban allure.

Central, often referred to as the financial hub of Hong Kong, boasts a mesmerizing skyline that showcases the city's architectural marvels. The district is punctuated by towering skyscrapers that reach towards the heavens, creating an awe-inspiring vista that defines the city's modernity. The iconic International Finance Centre (IFC) stands as a symbol of Central's financial prowess, housing global corporations and luxury shopping within its glass-clad walls. The IFC's rooftop garden provides a tranquil escape amidst the bustling urban environment, offering breathtaking views of Victoria Harbour.

Yet, amid the steel and glass, Central also offers a glimpse into Hong Kong's history and culture. Hidden alleyways and colonial-era buildings add a touch of nostalgia to the district. Strolling along Hollywood Road, visitors can explore antique shops, art galleries, and historic landmarks. The Man Mo Temple, an ancient Taoist temple, provides a serene oasis amidst the modern city, where incense smoke drifts among the intricate wooden carvings.

Adjacent to Central, Sheung Wan embraces a more laid-back atmosphere while still exuding an urban charm. This district is a microcosm of Hong Kong's cultural diversity, where traditional markets thrive alongside modern boutiques. The dried seafood and herbal medicine shops of Dried Seafood Street (Des Voeux Road West) create a sensory experience that immerses visitors in the city's trading heritage. In contrast, PMQ (Police Married Quarters), a former police dormitory turned creative hub, showcases local art, design, and craftsmanship.

Sheung Wan's culinary scene is equally diverse and tantalizing. Its streets are lined with eateries that cater to every palate, from traditional dim sum houses to trendy cafés serving fusion dishes. Gough Street and Tai Ping Shan Street offer a gastronomic journey through international flavors, while the vibrant Graham Street Market tempts visitors with fresh produce, aromatic spices, and street food.

Central and Sheung Wan share a convenient and well-connected transportation network that allows visitors to seamlessly explore the rest of Hong Kong. The Central-Mid-Levels Escalator, the world's longest outdoor covered escalator system, connects the districts and offers an unconventional mode of transportation through the city's hilly terrain. The Star Ferry, an iconic Hong Kong experience, provides a picturesque journey across Victoria Harbour, connecting Central to Tsim Sha Tsui on the Kowloon side.

or those seeking entertainment and cultural enrichment, the Fringe Club in Central hosts a ariety of artistic performances, from theater and music to exhibitions and workshops. In heung Wan, the heritage-rich Man Mo Temple often hosts traditional events and ceremonies, llowing visitors to witness the city's spiritual traditions in action.

Central and Sheung Wan embody Hong Kong's duality—where the past intertwines with the resent, and the modern coexists with tradition. The districts offer a multitude of experiences hat cater to diverse interests, from shopping and dining to history and art. Their seamless ntegration of different facets of city life makes Central and Sheung Wan a microcosm of Hong ong's vibrant and ever-evolving identity. It's a place where the pulse of the city can be felt, vhere the heartbeat of Hong Kong's urban charm resonates through every street, alley, and kyscraper.

Tsim Sha Tsui and Kowloon: A Vibrant Tapestry of Culture and Commerce

Jestled on the northern shores of Victoria Harbour, Tsim Sha Tsui and Kowloon form a bustling rban expanse that offers a captivating blend of culture, commerce, and history. These districts, ulsating with life and energy, provide a vivid snapshot of Hong Kong's dynamic character. rom iconic landmarks to vibrant markets, cultural institutions to modern shopping centers, sim Sha Tsui and Kowloon create a rich tapestry of experiences that resonate with both locals nd visitors alike.

sim Sha Tsui, often referred to simply as "TST," stands as a testament to Hong Kong's osmopolitan vibrancy. Its skyline is graced by some of the city's most recognizable landmarks, ncluding the towering skyscrapers of the International Commerce Centre (ICC) and the enowned cultural institution, the Hong Kong Space Museum. Nestled amid this modernity is

owloon Park, an urban oasis where visitors can find tranquility amidst the city's hustle and ustle.

t the heart of Tsim Sha Tsui lies the Avenue of Stars, a waterfront promenade that pays omage to Hong Kong's vibrant film industry. The promenade features handprints of local elebrities and offers stunning views of the iconic skyline across the harbor. Adjacent to this, he Tsim Sha Tsui Clock Tower stands as a historic relic of the city's past, serving as a reminder f its maritime heritage.

Kowloon, situated across the harbor from Hong Kong Island, embraces a unique blend of tradition and modernity. The district's streets are alive with the vibrant colors and enticing aromas of local markets, where vendors sell everything from exotic fruits and fresh seafood to traditional herbal remedies. The Ladies' Market, Temple Street Night Market, and Mong Kok's bustling streets offer a shopping experience that immerses visitors in the city's lively atmosphere.

Kowloon's rich cultural scene is equally captivating. The Kowloon Walled City Park pays homage to the district's history, showcasing remnants of the once densely populated and infamous Kowloon Walled City. The Hong Kong Museum of History offers a journey through the city's past, from ancient artifacts to modern exhibits that trace the evolution of Hong Kong's identity.

Tsim Sha Tsui and Kowloon's culinary landscape is a true reflection of Hong Kong's diverse culture. From traditional cha chaan tengs (local tea restaurants) serving classic dishes to upscale international eateries offering a fusion of flavors, the districts cater to every palate. The renowned Chungking Mansions is a melting pot of international cuisine, where visitors can sample dishes from around the world in a single complex.

For those seeking a blend of culture and entertainment, the Hong Kong Cultural Centre in Tsim Sha Tsui hosts a variety of artistic performances, including music, dance, theater, and exhibitions. In Kowloon, the iconic Symphony of Lights illuminates the skyline every evening, a synchronized spectacle of light and sound that celebrates the city's energy and diversity.

The districts are also well-connected by public transportation, allowing visitors to easily explore the rest of Hong Kong. The Star Ferry provides a picturesque journey across Victoria Harbour, offering breathtaking views of the skyline as it connects Tsim Sha Tsui to the Central district on Hong Kong Island. The MTR (Mass Transit Railway) system offers a quick and efficient way to navigate both Tsim Sha Tsui and Kowloon, as well as the wider city.

In conclusion, Tsim Sha Tsui and Kowloon are a vibrant tapestry of culture and commerce, history and modernity. Their iconic landmarks, bustling markets, cultural institutions, and diverse culinary offerings create an immersive experience that reflects the city's multifaceted identity. These districts are where Hong Kong's dynamic spirit shines brightest, where the heartbeat of the city can be felt through every bustling street, historic site, and cultural gem.

Tsim Sha Tsui and Kowloon stand as a testament to the city's ever-evolving character, offering a captivating snapshot of Hong Kong's rich heritage and vibrant present.

Causeway Bay and Wan Chai: Dynamic Urban Enclaves of Hong Kong

Nestled on the northern shore of Hong Kong Island, Causeway Bay and Wan Chai stand as vibrant urban enclaves that pulse with energy, commerce, and culture. These districts, each with its own distinct personality, offer a captivating blend of modernity, tradition, and entertainment that reflects the city's ever-evolving spirit. From bustling shopping centers to historic landmarks, art galleries to bustling markets, Causeway Bay and Wan Chai create a dynamic tapestry of experiences that resonates with both locals and visitors.

Causeway Bay, often touted as one of the world's most densely populated and vibrant neighborhoods, epitomizes Hong Kong's urban energy. This district boasts an impressive array of shopping centers, from the iconic Times Square with its vibrant LED displays to the luxurious shopping haven of Hysan Place. The district's streets are lined with international boutiques, department stores, and local shops that cater to every shopper's desire.

Beyond its shopping allure, Causeway Bay offers a myriad of culinary delights that showcase the city's diverse palate. Local cha chaan tengs (tea restaurants) serve up classic Hong Kong dishes, while trendy cafés and international eateries offer a fusion of flavors that cater to the city's cosmopolitan population. The district's energetic atmosphere extends to its dining scene, where visitors can savor everything from traditional dim sum to contemporary global cuisine.

Wan Chai, adjacent to Causeway Bay, presents a unique blend of history and modernity. The district is home to Hong Kong's vibrant arts and entertainment scene, with an array of galleries, theaters, and live music venues. The Hong Kong Arts Centre is a hub for creative expression, hosting exhibitions, performances, and cultural events that celebrate the city's artistic diversity.

The Star Street Precinct in Wan Chai offers a juxtaposition of old and new, with historic buildings transformed into trendy boutiques, cafés, and lifestyle shops. The district's traditional wet markets, such as the Tai Yuen Street Market, provide a glimpse into local daily life and offer fresh produce, seafood, and authentic street food.

Wan Chai's waterfront is graced by the iconic Hong Kong Convention and Exhibition Centre, a masterpiece of modern architecture that hosts international conferences, events, and exhibitions. The centre's distinctive glass façade and its backdrop of Victoria Harbour create a

striking visual that epitomizes Hong Kong's seamless blend of urban development and natural beauty.

For those seeking leisure and relaxation, Victoria Park in Causeway Bay offers an expansive green oasis where visitors can unwind, exercise, and enjoy scenic views. In Wan Chai, the historic Green House provides a tranquil space for visitors to immerse themselves in the district's colonial heritage and lush surroundings.

The districts are well-connected by public transportation, including the MTR (Mass Transit Railway) system, trams, and buses, allowing visitors to easily navigate the rest of Hong Kong. Additionally, the Wan Chai Star Ferry terminal offers a picturesque journey across Victoria Harbour, connecting Wan Chai to Tsim Sha Tsui on the Kowloon side.

In conclusion, Causeway Bay and Wan Chai are vibrant urban enclaves that encapsulate Hong Kong's dynamism, offering a seamless blend of modernity and tradition. Their bustling shopping scenes, diverse culinary offerings, cultural institutions, and green spaces create an immersive experience that reflects the city's multifaceted identity. These districts stand as a testament to Hong Kong's ability to harmonize its rich history and contemporary spirit, where every bustling street, historic landmark, and cultural gem pulsates with the vibrant heartbeat of the city. Causeway Bay and Wan Chai invite visitors to explore, engage, and embrace the dynamic tapestry of Hong Kong's past and present.

Lantau Island and Beyond: A Journey into Natural Beauty and Cultural Richness

Lantau Island, the largest outlying island in Hong Kong, stands as a sanctuary of natural beauty and cultural richness. As a stark contrast to the urban hustle of the city, Lantau offers a tranquil escape that resonates with both locals and visitors seeking respite from the fast-paced urban life. Beyond Lantau's shores, the surrounding islands and waters of the Hong Kong archipelago offer a journey into diverse landscapes, cultures, and experiences that celebrate the city's multifaceted identity.

Lantau Island is perhaps best known for its breathtaking landscapes and outdoor opportunities. The island's lush greenery, pristine beaches, and serene hiking trails make it a paradise for nature enthusiasts. The iconic Lantau Peak, the second-highest peak in Hong Kong, beckons adventurers to embark on a challenging hike that rewards with panoramic views of the island and the South China Sea. The Wisdom Path, a serene trail adorned with wooden prayer inscriptions, offers a meditative experience in the midst of nature's tranquility.

At the heart of Lantau Island lies Ngong Ping, a cultural and spiritual hub that houses the renowned Tian Tan Buddha, also known as the Big Buddha. This majestic bronze statue, surrounded by the Po Lin Monastery, stands as a symbol of enlightenment and offers a spiritual retreat for locals and pilgrims alike. A visit to the Ngong Ping 360 cable car offers a scenic ride that showcases the island's verdant landscapes and coastal vistas.

Exploring beyond Lantau Island, the surrounding islands of the Hong Kong archipelago provide an array of diverse experiences. From Lamma Island's relaxed beaches and seafood restaurants to Cheung Chau's traditional fishing village atmosphere, each island offers a unique charm that reflects Hong Kong's cultural diversity. The islands are connected by ferry services that provide an opportunity to hop between worlds, allowing visitors to immerse themselves in the slower pace of island life.

The UNESCO-listed Hong Kong Global Geopark spans across different islands and highlights the city's geological wonders. With unique rock formations, volcanic landscapes, and coastal features, the geopark provides an educational and visually stunning experience that showcases the earth's ancient history.

For those interested in marine life and underwater exploration, the waters surrounding Hong Kong are home to diverse marine ecosystems. The clear waters offer opportunities for snorkeling, diving, and marine tours that allow visitors to discover vibrant coral reefs, marine species, and underwater caves.

Culturally, Lantau Island and its neighboring islands offer a glimpse into Hong Kong's past and present. Traditional fishing villages, ancient temples, and ancestral halls stand as remnants of the city's heritage. The island's markets and local eateries allow visitors to savor authentic flavors and connect with the local way of life.

Lantau Island's proximity to Hong Kong International Airport positions it as a gateway for travelers arriving or departing from the city. The Airport Express train provides convenient transportation between Lantau and the city center, making it an ideal starting point for those looking to explore further.

In conclusion, Lantau Island and the surrounding islands offer a journey into natural beauty, cultural richness, and diverse experiences. From Lantau's serene landscapes and spiritual landmarks to the vibrant culture and marine wonders of the archipelago, these destinations provide a holistic view of Hong Kong's identity. Lantau and beyond invite visitors to discover the city's multifaceted allure, where the harmonious blend of nature, culture, and history creates an immersive experience that resonates with both locals and those seeking to explore the heart and soul of Hong Kong.

Section 6: Top Attractions

Victoria Peak: A Majestic Vista of Hong Kong's Splendor

Perched high above the bustling city of Hong Kong, Victoria Peak stands as an iconic vantage point that offers a majestic vista of the city's splendor. Affectionately known as "The Peak," this elevated viewpoint provides visitors with a breathtaking panoramic view of Hong Kong's dynamic skyline, shimmering harbor, and rolling landscapes. Beyond being a popular tourist attraction, Victoria Peak holds a special place in the hearts of both locals and visitors, offering an experience that captures the essence of the city's beauty and energy.

As one ascends the Peak, whether by the historic Peak Tram or the winding roads, a sense of anticipation builds. The journey itself is part of the adventure, with glimpses of the cityscape through the lush foliage that envelopes the route. Upon arrival, the awe-inspiring view that unfolds before visitors is nothing short of spectacular.

The panoramic vista from Victoria Peak showcases Hong Kong's captivating juxtaposition of urban development and natural beauty. The towering skyscrapers of Central and Admiralty juxtaposed against the tranquil waters of Victoria Harbour create a visual symphony of modernity and nature. The iconic International Finance Centre (IFC) and the glittering lights of the city come alive against the backdrop of the South China Sea.

As the sun sets over the horizon, the city transforms into a sea of glittering lights, forming a mesmerizing tapestry that extends as far as the eye can see. The Symphony of Lights, a nightly multimedia light and sound show that illuminates Hong Kong's skyline, adds an enchanting touch to the panorama. The city's vibrant energy is palpable from this elevated perch, where visitors can witness the pulse of Hong Kong in motion.

Victoria Peak offers more than just a visual spectacle; it is also home to various attractions and experiences that cater to diverse interests. The Peak Tower, an architectural marvel with its striking design, houses an array of shops, restaurants, and entertainment options. Sky Terrace 428, an outdoor observation deck, provides an unobstructed 360-degree view of the city and its surroundings, allowing visitors to immerse themselves in the city's grandeur.

Beyond the urban landscape, the Peak offers nature enthusiasts an opportunity to explore lush trails that wind through verdant forests. The Peak Circle Walk offers a tranquil escape, allowing hikers to enjoy the serene surroundings and take in stunning views from different angles. The

contrast between the city's urbanity and the island's natural beauty becomes evident as one traverses these scenic paths.

Victoria Peak's historical significance adds depth to its allure. Once a colonial escape from the heat and humidity, the Peak has transformed over the years into a cherished landmark that bridges the past and present. The historical Peak Tram, which has been in operation for over a century, provides a nostalgic journey to the summit, offering a glimpse into the city's evolution.

Local residents and visitors alike cherish Victoria Peak not only for its panoramic views but also for the sense of serenity it provides. As the city buzzes below, the Peak stands as a peaceful retreat, offering a space to reflect, admire, and capture the beauty of Hong Kong's diverse landscape.

In conclusion, Victoria Peak is a crown jewel that crowns Hong Kong's urban skyline, providing an unforgettable view of the city's splendor. With its panoramic vistas, historical significance, and tranquil natural surroundings, the Peak offers an experience that resonates with both locals and visitors seeking to embrace the heart and soul of Hong Kong. It is a destination that captures the essence of the city's dynamic spirit, allowing one to witness Hong Kong's grandeur from a perspective that is both humbling and awe-inspiring.

Hong Kong Disneyland: Where Dreams Come to Life

Nestled on Lantau Island, Hong Kong Disneyland stands as a magical gateway to imagination, enchantment, and the spirit of childhood wonder. This iconic theme park, part of the renowned Disney family of attractions, brings to life beloved characters, captivating stories, and immersive experiences that resonate with visitors of all ages. From its whimsical attractions to its enchanting entertainment, Hong Kong Disneyland offers a world where dreams come true and the magic of Disney is brought to life in the heart of Asia.

Upon entering Hong Kong Disneyland, visitors are transported into a realm where fantasy and reality intertwine seamlessly. The park's Main Street, U.S.A., welcomes guests with its charming architecture, colorful storefronts, and nostalgic ambiance, evoking the spirit of small-town America in a bygone era. As visitors stroll down Main Street, they are greeted by the friendly faces of Disney characters, setting the tone for a day filled with enchantment and joy.

The park Is divided into distinct themed lands that each offer a unique experience. Fantasyland, with its iconic Sleeping Beauty Castle as the centerpiece, invites guests to step into the enchanting worlds of classic Disney fairy tales. From spinning teacups in the Mad Hatter's Tea Cups to flying over Neverland on Peter Pan's Flight, Fantasyland allows visitors to relive timeless stories and create new memories.

Adventureland beckons explorers to embark on thrilling journeys through exotic locales. The Jungle River Cruise takes guests on a guided tour through lush jungles and mysterious rivers, encountering animatronic animals and unexpected surprises along the way. In Mystic Point, guests can embark on an interactive adventure in the Mystic Manor, a mansion filled with magical artifacts and whimsical curiosities.

Tomorrowland invites visitors to embrace the possibilities of the future and embark on high-tech adventures. The Iron Man Experience offers an immersive flight simulator that allows guests to join forces with Tony Stark and experience the thrill of being a superhero. Hyperspace Mountain catapults riders into a thrilling space battle, where they can engage in an epic Star Wars adventure.

Grizzly Gulch captures the spirit of the American frontier, inviting guests to embark on a runaway mine car adventure through a scenic landscape filled with surprises. Toy Story Land transports visitors into the whimsical world of toys, where oversized props and beloved characters from the Toy Story franchise come to life in a playful and vibrant environment.

Beyond its attractions, Hong Kong Disneyland offers a wide range of entertainment options that captivate and delight. The stage comes alive with captivating musicals, parades, and fireworks that showcase Disney's signature storytelling and entertainment prowess. These experiences create a sense of wonder and connection, allowing guests to immerse themselves in the magic of Disney's beloved characters and stories.

The park's commitment to guest satisfaction is evident in its attention to detail, customer service, and accessibility. Hong Kong Disneyland ensures that visitors have a seamless and enjoyable experience, from providing a variety of dining options to accommodating the needs of families and individuals with diverse backgrounds.

Hong Kong Disneyland is not just a theme park; it's a place where cherished memories are made, where families bond, and where the spirit of imagination thrives. Its unique blend of Disney magic, cultural relevance, and awe-inspiring attractions make it a beloved destination for both locals and international visitors seeking to experience the enchantment of Disney in the heart of Asia.

In conclusion, Hong Kong Disneyland stands as a testament to the power of imagination, storytelling, and the magic of Disney. Through its themed lands, attractions, entertainment, and attention to detail, the park brings to life the cherished characters and stories that have captured the hearts of generations. It is a place where dreams come to life, where visitors of all ages can rediscover the joy of childhood and create memories that last a lifetime. Hong Kong

Disneyland is more than a theme park; it's a place where the enchantment of Disney's world comes alive, reminding us that the magic of imagination knows no boundaries.

Tian Tan Buddha: A Symbol of Spiritual Serenity and Cultural Significance

Nestled atop the lush green hills of Lantau Island, the Tian Tan Buddha, also known as the Big Buddha, stands as an iconic symbol of spiritual serenity and cultural significance in Hong Kong. This majestic bronze statue, surrounded by the serene Po Lin Monastery, captures the essence of Buddhist teachings and offers a sanctuary for locals and visitors alike seeking solace, enlightenment, and a deeper connection to the spiritual heritage of the region.

As visitors ascend the steps leading to the Tian Tan Buddha, a sense of reverence and awe washes over them. The statue, perched at a height of 34 meters (112 feet), is a sight to behold, exuding an air of tranquility and wisdom. The statue's serene expression and poised demeanor reflect the core principles of Buddhism—compassion, wisdom, and inner peace. The Buddha's right hand is raised in a gesture known as the "abhaya mudra," symbolizing fearlessness and protection, while the left hand rests gently on his lap, representing meditation and inner tranquility.

The Tian Tan Buddha was unveiled in 1993, a profound milestone in celebrating Hong Kong's religious diversity and cultural heritage. The statue was meticulously cast in bronze, with each intricate detail and contour capturing the essence of traditional Buddhist artistry. The significance of its construction extends beyond its physical form; it represents a fusion of spirituality, art, and cultural expression.

Surrounded by the Po Lin Monastery, the Tian Tan Buddha holds a central place in the religious landscape of Hong Kong. The monastery, founded in 1906, is a place of deep reverence and meditation, where Buddhist monks and devotees come to practice, reflect, and seek spiritual enlightenment. Its ornate architecture, vibrant decorations, and serene atmosphere create an environment that encourages introspection and connection with the divine.

The journey to the Tian Tan Buddha is not just a physical one; it is a spiritual pilgrimage that invites visitors to pause, reflect, and contemplate. The Ngong Ping 360 cable car ride, offering breathtaking views of Lantau's landscapes, serves as a prelude to the spiritual experience awaiting atop the hill. The path leading to the Buddha, flanked by statues depicting celestial guardians, mirrors the journey of self-discovery and purification that Buddhism advocates.

The panoramic view from the Tian Tan Buddha's platform is nothing short of spectacular. Visitors are treated to sweeping vistas of Lantau's rolling hills, lush forests, and the shimmering waters of the South China Sea. The breathtaking beauty of the surroundings fosters a sense of unity with nature and underscores the interconnectedness of all living beings—a fundamental principle in Buddhist philosophy.

Beyond its spiritual significance, the Tian Tan Buddha has become a beacon of cultural tourism, drawing both locals and international visitors seeking to explore Hong Kong's diverse cultural landscape. The statue's prominence has solidified it as one of the city's most beloved landmarks, a place where spirituality and cultural heritage converge.

As day turns into night, the Tian Tan Buddha takes on a new dimension. Illuminated against the backdrop of the darkening sky, the statue radiates a serene glow that resonates with the inner light and wisdom Buddhism seeks to awaken within each individual. The tranquil ambiance fosters a sense of connection to something greater—a universal consciousness that transcends borders, beliefs, and backgrounds.

In conclusion, the Tian Tan Buddha stands as a powerful symbol of spiritual serenity, cultural significance, and timeless wisdom in Hong Kong. Its presence atop Lantau Island serves as a reminder of the universal human quest for understanding, enlightenment, and inner peace. The statue's fusion of artistic craftsmanship, spiritual philosophy, and natural beauty creates a space that transcends the boundaries of religion and culture, inviting all to embrace the essence of the teachings it embodies. The Tian Tan Buddha is not just a monument; it's a beacon of hope, a testament to the enduring pursuit of truth, and a source of inspiration for all who seek to discover the profound depths of their own souls.

The Star Ferry: A Timeless Connection Across Victoria Harbour

Amid the towering skyscrapers and bustling urban landscape of Hong Kong, the Star Ferry stands as a cherished emblem of the city's history, resilience, and enduring spirit. For more than a century, this iconic ferry service has provided a timeless connection across Victoria Harbour, serving as a lifeline for commuters, a link between Hong Kong Island and Kowloon, and a symbol of the city's progress and unity.

From its humble beginnings in the late 19th century, the Star Ferry has evolved into a cultural institution that transcends generations. The service traces its roots back to 1880 when local entrepreneur Dorabjee Naorojee Mithaiwala introduced a simple rowing boat to transport

passengers across the harbor. Over time, the fleet grew, and the Star Ferry Company was established, solidifying its role as an integral part of Hong Kong's transport network.

Today, the Star Ferry's fleet includes modern vessels that offer both efficiency and nostalgia. The iconic green and white boats, with their distinctive bow designs, continue to traverse the harbor, providing a scenic journey that bridges the gap between Hong Kong Island and Kowloon. The Star Ferry experience is not merely a mode of transportation; it's a living link to the past, a portal to breathtaking views, and a testament to the city's unwavering connection to its maritime heritage.

The crossing between Central and Tsim Sha Tsui offers passengers a front-row seat to Hong Kong's ever-changing skyline. As the ferry glides across the tranquil waters, passengers are treated to panoramic vistas that capture the essence of the city's contrasts—where modern skyscrapers meet the historic remnants of Victoria Harbour's maritime past. The journey offers a perspective that allows passengers to witness the harmonious blend of past and present that defines Hong Kong's identity.

Beyond its visual appeal, the Star Ferry experience evokes a sense of nostalgia and connection to history. The rhythmic sound of the engines, the gentle sway of the boat, and the salty breeze that caresses one's skin create an immersive experience that transports passengers to a bygone era. It's a feeling of timelessness that carries with it a sense of reverence for the generations that have traversed these waters before.

The Star Ferry's cultural significance goes beyond its role as a means of transport. It has become a symbol of Hong Kong's resilience, adaptability, and unity. The ferry continued to operate even during challenging times, including World War II and moments of political uncertainty, demonstrating its importance as a lifeline that binds communities on both sides of the harbor.

The Star Ferry's contribution to Hong Kong's cultural fabric extends to the realm of art and literature. Its iconic silhouette has inspired countless artists, writers, and filmmakers to capture its essence as a symbol of the city's spirit. The ferry's legacy is woven into the narratives that have shaped Hong Kong's identity, reflecting themes of journeys, connections, and the ebb and flow of life.

To the people of Hong Kong, the Star Ferry is more than just a mode of transportation—it's a source of pride, a testament to the city's resilience, and a cherished memory that resonates with generations. Locals and visitors alike find solace in the familiarity of the ferry's chime and the embrace of its timeless voyage. The Star Ferry's ability to evoke a sense of nostalgia while remaining relevant in the modern world is a testament to its enduring legacy.

In conclusion, the Star Ferry stands as a living testament to Hong Kong's history, culture, and resilience. Its crossing across Victoria Harbour is more than a commute; it's a journey through time and space, a visual ode to the city's vibrant spirit, and a poignant reminder of the city's maritime roots. As the Star Ferry continues to ferry passengers across the waters that have shaped Hong Kong's identity, it remains a bridge between the past and the present, a vessel of stories and memories, and an enduring symbol of the city's soul.

Avenue of Stars: Honoring Legends, Celebrating Cinema

In the heart of the vibrant cityscape of Tsim Sha Tsui, Hong Kong, the Avenue of Stars stands as a tribute to the iconic figures who have shaped the city's cinematic legacy. Much more than a simple promenade, this glittering walkway offers a unique blend of cultural homage, breathtaking views, and a celebration of Hong Kong's influence on the global film industry. From its dedication to legendary stars to its stunning backdrop of Victoria Harbour, the Avenue of Stars weaves together the threads of art, culture, and entertainment that have defined the spirit of the city.

Inspired by the Hollywood Walk of Fame, the Avenue of Stars pays homage to the luminaries of Hong Kong cinema who have left an indelible mark on the world stage. As visitors stroll along the walkway, they encounter the handprints, signatures, and statues of iconic actors and actresses who have graced both local and international screens. These enduring figures, from Bruce Lee to Jackie Chan, Anita Mui to Maggie Cheung, represent a rich tapestry of talent that has captivated audiences across the globe.

The centerpiece of the Avenue of Stars is the bronze statue of Bruce Lee, an internationally acclaimed martial artist and actor who remains an enduring cultural icon. With his characteristic pose frozen in bronze, Lee's statue stands as a symbol of determination, discipline, and the city's cinematic prowess. The statue's location against the backdrop of Victoria Harbour adds an element of grandeur, encapsulating the symbiotic relationship between Hong Kong's cinematic heritage and its stunning natural beauty.

The Avenue of Stars is not merely a static tribute; it comes alive with various interactive features and multimedia displays that engage and educate visitors. The Hong Kong Film Award Experiences showcase the glamour of the city's film industry through exhibits and memorabilia allowing visitors to delve into the world of filmmaking, costume design, and cinematic history. The experience offers a glimpse into the creative process behind some of Hong Kong's most celebrated films.

As day turns into night, the Avenue of Stars transforms into a mesmerizing spectacle. The Symphony of Lights, a synchronized light and sound show that illuminates the city's skyline, dazzles viewers with its choreographed display of color and movement. The dazzling show, ecognized by Guinness World Records as the world's "largest permanent light and sound show," adds an enchanting layer to the already captivating ambiance of the promenade.

Beyond its cinematic homage, the Avenue of Stars offers unparalleled views of Victoria Harbour and the Hong Kong skyline. As the sun dips below the horizon, the cityscape comes alive with the glittering lights of skyscrapers, creating a picturesque scene that reflects the city's vibrant energy. Visitors are treated to a breathtaking panoramic view that encapsulates the city's modernity and the timeless allure of the harbor.

The Avenue of Stars also plays a significant role in fostering cultural connections and community engagement. It serves as a venue for a variety of events, from outdoor film screenings to live performances, that celebrate the arts and bring people together. Its location along the harbor promenade encourages both locals and visitors to gather, connect, and share in the city's creative spirit.

In essence, the Avenue of Stars is more than a walkway—it's a living testament to the artistic heritage, cultural diversity, and cinematic excellence that define Hong Kong. It pays homage to the individuals who have contributed to the city's legacy while simultaneously offering a platform for the arts to thrive. The Avenue of Stars represents a harmonious convergence of past and present, of creative expression and natural beauty, creating an experience that is both enlightening and enchanting.

In conclusion, the Avenue of Stars is a cultural gem that weaves together the threads of Hong Kong's cinematic legacy, natural splendor, and creative vitality. Its dedication to legendary figures, its captivating multimedia displays, and its breathtaking views make it a dynamic and immersive destination for both film enthusiasts and casual visitors alike. As visitors stroll along the promenade, they become part of a larger narrative—a narrative that celebrates the enduring impact of cinema, the vibrant spirit of Hong Kong, and the magical interplay between art and life.

Ocean Park: Where Conservation, Entertainment, and Nature Converge

Nestled on the southern coast of Hong Kong Island, Ocean Park stands as a beacon of entertainment, education, and conservation that harmoniously blends the wonders of nature with exhilarating attractions. For decades, this iconic theme park and marine life center has captured the hearts of locals and visitors alike, offering a unique blend of thrill, discovery, and a commitment to the preservation of marine and terrestrial ecosystems.

As visitors step into Ocean Park, they are immediately enveloped in a world that celebrates the beauty of the ocean and the diversity of life it sustains. The park's two main areas, the Waterfront and the Summit, provide a spectrum of experiences that cater to a wide range of interests. From breathtaking marine exhibits to adrenaline-pumping rides, Ocean Park offers an immersive journey that bridges the gap between entertainment and education.

One of Ocean Park's hallmarks is its dedication to marine conservation and education. The Grand Aquarium, a mesmerizing underwater world, showcases vibrant coral reefs, exotic fish species, and the intricate balance of marine ecosystems. The park's conservation efforts extend to the Ocean Theatre, where visitors are treated to captivating dolphin and sea lion shows that highlight the intelligence and agility of these majestic creatures while also raising awareness about their conservation status.

Beyond its marine exhibits, Ocean Park's commitment to environmental education is evident in its various educational programs and exhibits. The Giant Panda Adventure, for instance, provides visitors with the opportunity to observe and learn about the endangered giant pandas and their habitats. The park's partnership with the Chengdu Research Base of Giant Panda Breeding underscores its dedication to global conservation initiatives.

Ocean Park seamlessly transitions from educational exploration to heart-pounding excitement with its thrilling rides and attractions. The Hair Raiser roller coaster offers an adrenaline rush as it twists and turns along the park's coast, offering panoramic views of the South China Sea. The Abyss, a vertical drop ride, provides an exhilarating freefall experience that challenges even the bravest of adventurers.

For families and children, Ocean Park presents an array of interactive zones and attractions. Whiskers Harbour offers a playful space where young visitors can enjoy rides, meet beloved characters, and participate in interactive games that nurture their imagination and creativity. The Polar Adventure area transports visitors to the Arctic and Antarctic regions, allowing them to encounter adorable animals such as penguins and seals.

The harmony between entertainment and nature is beautifully exemplified In Ocean Park's Cable Car system. The cable car ride offers breathtaking views of the park's lush landscapes, marine exhibits, and the picturesque surroundings of Hong Kong Island. As visitors glide above the treetops and over the ocean, they are reminded of the symbiotic relationship between humanity and the natural world.

The park's Iconic Ocean Express funicular railway further enhances the immersive experience, providing visitors with an underwater journey from the Waterfront to the Summit. The ride simulates a submarine voyage, complete with mesmerizing aquatic scenes that offer a glimpse into the underwater realm.

Ocean Park's commitment to sustainability is evident in its efforts to reduce its ecological footprint and promote eco-friendly practices. The park's solar power initiatives, waste reduction programs, and sustainable dining options showcase its dedication to environmental responsibility. By incorporating eco-friendly practices into its operations, Ocean Park sets an example for visitors and demonstrates that entertainment and conservation can coexist harmoniously.

In conclusion, Ocean Park is a remarkable testament to the convergence of entertainment, conservation, and education. It offers a dynamic blend of thrills, marine wonders, and immersive experiences that capture the essence of Hong Kong's natural beauty and cultural diversity. From its commitment to marine conservation to its exhilarating rides and educational exhibits, Ocean Park creates a space where entertainment, learning, and nature come together to inspire, educate, and entertain visitors of all ages. It serves as a reminder that through conscious efforts, humans can coexist with the natural world while appreciating its majesty and protecting its future.

Section 7: Dining

Local Cuisine and Food Markets

Hong Kong, renowned for its culinary diversity and rich food culture, offers a tantalizing array of local cuisine and bustling food markets that cater to both traditional palates and adventurous eaters. From bustling street markets to iconic dim sum parlors, the city's food scene is a vibrant tapestry that reflects its multicultural heritage. Here are some of the best local cuisine and food markets that capture the essence of Hong Kong's culinary delights:

Dim Dim Sum Dim Sum Specialty SStor: For an authentic dim sum experience, Dim Dim Sum is a must-visit. This bustling restaurant offers a wide variety of bite-sized delicacies, from steamed dumplings to fluffy buns filled with savory and sweet fillings. Dim sum is not just a meal; it's a cultural experience, and Dim Dim Sum delivers with its quality and diversity.

Temple Street Night Market: This iconic night market is not only a treasure trove of knick-knacks and souvenirs but also a paradise for street food enthusiasts. As the sun sets, the market comes alive with food stalls offering everything from seafood skewers and clay pot rice to spicy noodles and delectable desserts. Temple Street Night Market is where you can truly immerse yourself in Hong Kong's street food culture.

Tai O Fishing Village: For a taste of traditional seafood, Tai O Fishing Village is a hidden gem. This charming village is famous for its stilt houses and seafood markets. Visitors can savor freshly caught seafood, such as salted fish, dried shrimp, and the iconic "pink shrimp paste," a local delicacy used in various dishes.

Sai Kung Seafood Street: Nestled in the seaside town of Sai Kung, this vibrant street is lined with seafood restaurants offering an array of delectable dishes. You can handpick live seafood from the tanks and have it cooked to your liking. From mouthwatering crab dishes to succulent prawns, Sai Kung Seafood Street promises an unforgettable culinary adventure.

Graham Street Market: This bustling wet market in Central provides a glimpse into Hong Kong's daily life and culinary culture. Fresh produce, herbs, spices, and an assortment of ingredients are on display, offering an authentic experience of local market shopping. Exploring Graham Street Market is an opportunity to connect with the city's culinary roots.

Yum Cha: Known for its playful and inventive take on traditional dim sum, Yum Cha is a trendy spot that fuses culinary artistry with classic flavors. Their delightful dim sum creations, shaped like adorable animals and objects, make for a whimsical and delicious dining experience.

Mak's Noodle: When it comes to quintessential Hong Kong comfort food, wonton noodles take the spotlight. Mak's Noodle is renowned for its delicate wonton dumplings and springy noodles served in a clear and flavorful broth. This humble noodle shop has a legacy dating back to the 1920s and continues to impress with its time-honored recipe.

Hong Kong Egg Waffles (Gai Dan Jai): These iconic street snacks are a delight for both the eyes and the palate. The crispy yet fluffy texture of the egg waffles, coupled with their distinctive honeycomb pattern, makes them a beloved treat. They come in a variety of flavors, from classic to matcha and even chocolate.

Mui Kee Congee: Congee, a rice porridge dish, holds a special place in Hong Kong's food culture. Mui Kee Congee is renowned for its silky-smooth congee, prepared with meticulous care and served with a variety of toppings. This humble eatery highlights the beauty of simple, well-executed dishes.

Wan Chai Market: This vibrant wet market offers a sensory feast of fresh produce, meats, seafood, and condiments. It's a wonderful place to witness the locals' daily routine and to explore the ingredients that contribute to Hong Kong's diverse cuisine.

In conclusion, Hong Kong's culinary landscape is a melting pot of flavors, traditions, and cultures. From iconic street snacks to bustling food markets, the city invites visitors to embark on a gastronomic journey that reveals the heart and soul of its food culture. Whether you're exploring vibrant markets or indulging in mouthwatering local specialties, the diverse range of options ensures that every palate is satisfied and every meal is an adventure.

Dim Dim Sum Dim Sum Specialty Store: A Culinary Odyssey of Flavors and Traditions

In the heart of the bustling culinary landscape of Hong Kong, Dim Dim Sum Dim Sum Specialty Store stands as a culinary gem that captures the essence of traditional dim sum while infusing it with modern creativity and artistry. As one of the city's beloved dining destinations, this unassuming eatery has carved a niche for itself by reimagining classic dim sum dishes and delivering a sensory experience that transports diners to a realm of flavors, textures, and cultural richness.

Nestled amidst the lively streets of Mong Kok, Dim Dim Sum stands as a testament to the enduring popularity of dim sum—a cherished culinary tradition that has transcended generations and borders. As visitors step into the cozy interior of the restaurant, they are welcomed by an ambiance that exudes both warmth and authenticity. The scent of freshly steamed dumplings and the gentle hum of conversation create an atmosphere that invites patrons to immerse themselves in the culinary journey that lies ahead.

The heart and soul of Dim Dim Sum lie in its diverse and meticulously crafted menu. The menu pays homage to the traditional art of dim sum making while incorporating playful twists that showcase the culinary team's creativity. From the moment the menu is placed in your hands, you are presented with an array of choices that promise to tantalize the taste buds and offer a symphony of flavors.

One of the quintessential delights of dim sum is the variety it offers, and Dim Dim Sum takes this concept to new heights. From the moment the first dish arrives, it becomes evident that every bite is a manifestation of culinary craftsmanship. Each plate is a canvas that tells a story of dedication, innovation, and a commitment to preserving the authentic essence of dim sum.

The signature dishes at Dim Dim Sum embody the restaurant's philosophy of blending tradition with innovation. The iconic Har Gow (shrimp dumplings) appear as delicate parcels of translucent perfection, showcasing the mastery required to achieve the ideal balance of wrapper and filling. Siew Mai (pork dumplings) are presented with a twist, featuring colorful wrappers that add a playful touch to the classic dish.

The fusion of flavors Is evident in dishes like the Truffle and Mushroom Bun, where the earthy aroma of truffle harmonizes with the savory notes of the mushroom filling. The Char Siu Bao (barbecue pork bun), a staple in dim sum cuisine, is elevated with a rich and tender filling that embodies the epitome of comfort food.

One cannot discuss dim sum without acknowledging the role of dumplings, and Dim Dim Sum does justice to this cherished tradition. The restaurant's Xiao Long Bao (soup dumplings) are a testament to the chef's skill in crafting delicate wrappers that encase a burst of flavorful broth and tender meat. With each bite, you embark on a sensory journey that encompasses taste, aroma, and texture.

The dessert offerings at Dim Dim Sum are equally tantalizing, showcasing the restaurant's commitment to providing a well-rounded dining experience. The Molten Salted Egg Yolk Buns, a contemporary twist on traditional custard buns, offer a luscious and indulgent surprise as the molten filling oozes out with the first bite.

The charm of Dim Dim Sum extends beyond its culinary offerings; it embodies the spirit of communal dining that is intrinsic to dim sum culture. Sharing a variety of dishes with friends and family is not just a meal—it's an experience that fosters connections, conversations, and the joy of discovering new flavors together.

In conclusion, Dim Dim Sum Dim Sum Specialty Store is a culinary haven that captures the heart of dim sum culture while embracing innovation and artistry. It pays homage to the traditional craft of dim sum making while delighting diners with inventive twists that evoke a sense of wonder. The restaurant's dedication to both authenticity and creativity ensures that every visit is a journey through the rich tapestry of Hong Kong's culinary heritage. As you savor each bite and share in the communal joy of dining, you're reminded that Dim Dim Sum is not just a restaurant—it's a celebration of flavors, traditions, and the timeless pleasure of sharing a meal with loved ones.

Temple Street Night Market: A Kaleidoscope of Culture, Commerce, and Culinary Delights

As the sun dips below the horizon, a vibrant transformation takes place on the streets of Hong Kong. The bustling energy of the day gives way to the enchanting allure of the night, and nowhere is this transformation more vividly experienced than at the Temple Street Night Market. Nestled in the heart of Kowloon's Yau Ma Tei district, this iconic market is a captivating symphony of lights, aromas, and sounds that beckon visitors to immerse themselves in a world of culture, commerce, and culinary delights.

Stepping into the Temple Street Night Market is akin to entering a portal to a different era—a time when the art of haggling, the camaraderie of shared exploration, and the intimacy of street life converged to create a dynamic and lively atmosphere. The market's vibrant façade is awash with colorful neon signs that illuminate the night sky, casting a mesmerizing glow over the bustling scene below.

Stretching along the eponymous Temple Street, the market sprawls with an eclectic array of stalls and vendors that offer everything from trinkets and clothing to electronics and antiques. As you navigate through the labyrinth of goods on display, you're transported into a treasure trove of curiosities, each item carrying with it a story of craftsmanship, history, and cultural significance. From intricate porcelain figurines to vintage watches, the market's offerings reflect the kaleidoscope of interests and tastes that converge within its bustling alleys.

One of the market's defining features is its emphasis on the art of negotiation—a time-honored tradition that adds a layer of excitement to the shopping experience. Engaging in friendly banter with the vendors, honing your bargaining skills, and reaching a mutually satisfying price are all part of the Temple Street Night Market ritual. It's a dance of wit and humor, where buyers and sellers forge connections through shared exchanges and spirited negotiations.

Amidst the sea of goods, a harmonious cacophony of sounds fills the air. The market is alive with the melodies of street performers, the rhythmic clatter of mahjong tiles, and the laughter of friends and families enjoying each other's company. Fortune tellers offer insights into the future, while local artists showcase their talents through live demonstrations and exhibitions. Every corner of the market invites you to engage with the culture and spirit of Hong Kong in a unique and immersive manner.

No exploration of Temple Street Night Market is complete without indulging in its culinary offerings. The aroma of sizzling skewers, aromatic spices, and savoring sauces permeates the air, enticing your taste buds and guiding you toward the delectable street food stalls that line the market's pathways. From succulent seafood skewers and piping hot curry fish balls to mouthwatering noodles and exotic fruits, the market is a gastronomic adventure that celebrates the diverse flavors of Hong Kong.

At the heart of the market lies its food stalls, where skilled vendors skillfully prepare and serve an array of local favorites. The Clay Pot Rice, a hearty and aromatic dish featuring rice, meat, and vegetables cooked in a clay pot, embodies the comfort and heartiness of Hong Kong cuisine. For those seeking a bold and savory experience, the stinky tofu—known for its pungent aroma and distinctive taste—offers a truly unique culinary encounter.

Beyond the sensory indulgence, Temple Street Night Market carries with it a sense of community and shared heritage. Locals and tourists alike gather here to partake in the market's lively atmosphere, creating a sense of belonging and camaraderie that transcends language and backgrounds. The market serves as a bridge that unites individuals from different walks of life, fostering connections and interactions that showcase the city's cosmopolitan spirit.

In conclusion, the Temple Street Night Market is a captivating tapestry that weaves together culture, commerce, and culinary experiences under the starlit sky. It is a celebration of tradition and modernity, a convergence of heritage and innovation, and a reminder of the enduring charm of street life. Whether you're shopping for unique treasures, engaging in friendly negotiations, or savoring the diverse flavors of Hong Kong street food, the market invites you to embrace the magic of the night and become part of a centuries-old tradition that continues to thrive in the heart of the city. As you wander through the market's illuminated alleyways and immerse yourself in its vibrant tapestry, you're reminded that the Temple Street Night Market is not just a place—it's an experience, a memory, and a testament to the timeless allure of the night.

Tai O Fishing Village: A Tranquil Journey Through Time and Tradition

Nestled along the tranquil shores of Lantau Island in Hong Kong, the Tai O Fishing Village stands as a living testament to the city's maritime heritage and the enduring connection between its residents and the sea. As one of the last remaining traditional fishing villages in Hong Kong, Tai O offers a captivating journey through time, providing a glimpse into a way of life that has remained unchanged for generations. With its stilt houses, bustling markets, and the rhythmic ebb and flow of daily life, Tai O invites visitors to step back in time and immerse themselves in the timeless charm of a bygone era.

The village's most distinctive feature is its stilt houses, a hallmark of the fishing communities that once dotted the coastlines of Hong Kong. These houses, built above the water on sturdy stilts, create a captivating visual spectacle as they reflect in the gentle ripples of the sea. The sight of these stilt houses, connected by narrow walkways and interconnected bridges, evokes a sense of nostalgia and serenity, offering a stark contrast to the modern cityscape that defines much of Hong Kong.

As visitors meander through the labyrinthine alleys of Tai O, they're met with an ambiance that resonates with the echoes of the past. The scent of saltwater mingles with the aromas of freshly caught seafood, creating an olfactory tapestry that captures the essence of village life. The friendly greetings of residents and the gentle clatter of daily activities reflect a sense of community that thrives amidst the simplicity of daily routines.

Tai O's traditional character is perhaps most evident in its vibrant markets, where local vendors showcase their wares and fresh catches. The Tai O Market offers a delightful array of seafood, dried goods, and local produce that reflect the village's deep connection to the sea. From salted fish and dried shrimp to preserved fruits and traditional snacks, the market exudes an authenticity that transports visitors to a time when such trades were the lifeblood of the community.

One of the village's most cherished traditions is its fishing culture, which remains integral to the livelihoods of many residents. Fishing boats bob gently in the harbor, bearing witness to the unbreakable bond between the villagers and the sea. Local fishermen set out in the early hours, casting their nets and traps in a dance that harmonizes with the rhythm of the tides. The symbiotic relationship between the villagers and the ocean is a poignant reminder of the respect and resilience required to live in harmony with nature.

A visit to Tai O would be incomplete without indulging in its culinary offerings, particularly its seafood delicacies. The village is renowned for its distinctive flavors, ranging from freshly grilled seafood skewers to renowned shrimp paste—a staple of Tai O cuisine. The opportunity to savor seafood that has been harvested from the waters just beyond the stilt houses is an experience that embodies the essence of Tai O's maritime culture.

While Tai O is steeped in tradition, it also embraces modernity in ways that complement its historic charm. The Tai O Heritage Hotel, once a police station, has been transformed into a boutique hotel that offers guests a unique blend of history and comfort. Visitors can explore the hotel's exhibits to gain insight into the village's past, further enhancing their understanding of its cultural significance.

In conclusion, Tai O Fishing Village is a treasure trove of heritage, culture, and authenticity that encapsulates the spirit of Hong Kong's maritime legacy. As you wander through its stilt houses, engage with its residents, and savor its culinary delights, you embark on a tranquil journey through time that transports you to an era when life was intimately intertwined with the rhythms of the sea. Tai O's ability to preserve its traditions while embracing its evolution is a testament to its enduring significance as a cultural gem that stands as a bridge between the past and the present, offering a unique glimpse into the soul of Hong Kong.

Sai Kung Seafood Street: A Gastronomic Odyssey of Freshness and Flavor

Nestled along the picturesque shores of Sai Kung, a charming coastal town in the northeastern part of Hong Kong, Sai Kung Seafood Street stands as a culinary haven that celebrates the bounties of the sea. With its bustling seafood markets, eclectic dining options, and breathtaking waterfront views, this vibrant street offers a gastronomic odyssey that transports visitors into a world of maritime flavors, cultural richness, and culinary delight.

The allure of Sai Kung Seafood Street lies In its unique blend of authenticity and variety. As you step onto the vibrant street, you're greeted by the captivating aroma of the sea and the colorful displays of seafood that beckon from the market stalls. The street is a haven for seafood enthusiasts, an immersive experience that not only allows you to savor the finest catches but also invites you to witness the essence of the fishing industry and the intricate processes that bring the ocean's bounty to your plate.

The bustling seafood markets of Sai Kung Seafood Street offer a sensory overload of sights and sounds that encapsulate the essence of a traditional fishing village. Vendors proudly display their freshly caught treasures—vibrant prawns, succulent crabs, gleaming fish, and a diverse array of shellfish—all harvested from the surrounding waters. The market's atmosphere is alive with the calls of vendors, the clatter of utensils, and the chatter of visitors, creating an ambiance that is equal parts vibrant and authentic.

One of the defining features of Sai Kung Seafood Street is its interactive dining experience. Upon selecting your desired seafood, you have the option to have it cooked to your preference at the nearby restaurants. This unique process ensures the utmost freshness and flavor, as the seafood goes from the ocean to your plate in the shortest possible time. This farm-to-table concept highlights the importance of quality and highlights the respect for the ingredients that is deeply ingrained in the local culinary culture.

The street's array of seafood restaurants offers a spectrum of culinary experiences, from rustic open-air eateries to cozy indoor establishments. Each restaurant boasts its own menu, with a variety of dishes that cater to different palates and preferences. From mouthwatering grilled prawns marinated with garlic and butter to aromatic seafood stews bursting with local herbs and spices, every dish is a symphony of flavors that reflect the seafood's natural richness.

Sai Kung Seafood Street also celebrates the art of communal dining, a practice that is deeply rooted in Asian culinary culture. Families, friends, and visitors gather around the tables to share an assortment of dishes, creating an atmosphere of togetherness and conviviality. The dining experience is elevated by the stunning waterfront views that Sai Kung offers, adding an element of natural beauty to the sensory feast.

The street's seafood offerings extend beyond the fresh catches to encompass an array of culinary techniques and flavors. From traditional Cantonese preparations that emphasize the natural taste of the ingredients to fusion dishes that infuse international influences, the street caters to a diverse range of tastes. Whether you're savoring a classic steamed fish with ginger and soy sauce or indulging in innovative seafood pasta creations, each dish showcases the creativity and adaptability of the culinary scene.

Sai Kung Seafood Street is more than just a place to enjoy a meal; it's a journey that encapsulates the spirit of Sai Kung's maritime heritage and the culinary passion of its residents. Beyond the delectable flavors, it offers an immersion into the heart of a coastal community, where the relationship between the sea and the people is celebrated with every bite. As you explore the market, interact with the vendors, and savor the sumptuous seafood offerings, you become part of a narrative that pays homage to the ocean's generosity, the village's traditions, and the joy of savoring the treasures of the sea.

Graham Street Market: A Culinary Tapestry of Heritage and Diversity

Nestled within the heart of Hong Kong's bustling Central district, Graham Street Market is a vibrant tapestry that weaves together the threads of tradition, community, and culinary diversity. As one of the city's oldest and most iconic street markets, Graham Street Market offers a sensory journey that showcases the rich flavors, vibrant colors, and vibrant spirit of Hong Kong's local culinary scene.

From the moment you step into Graham Street Market, you're greeted by a lively atmosphere that captures the essence of Hong Kong's dynamic street culture. The market's narrow alleys are brimming with life, as vendors proudly display their wares, creating a kaleidoscope of color that range from the vibrant hues of fresh produce to the rich tones of aromatic spices. The market's energy is infectious, drawing you in with its bustling ambiance and inviting you to explore its hidden treasures.

One of the defining characteristics of Graham Street Market is its role as a culinary crossroads, where flavors from around the world converge to create a diverse and eclectic dining experience. The market's offerings reflect the multicultural fabric of Hong Kong, with stalls that cater to a wide range of palates and preferences. From traditional Cantonese dishes to international street food, Graham Street Market is a haven for food enthusiasts seeking an authentic taste of the city's culinary landscape.

Freshness is the hallmark of Graham Street Market's produce, and it's evident in every stall and every ingredient on display. The market boasts an impressive array of fruits, vegetables, and herbs, all sourced from local farms and delivered daily to ensure the highest quality. As you stroll through the market, you're greeted by the vibrant colors of juicy tropical fruits, crisp leafy greens, and fragrant herbs that reflect the vitality of Hong Kong's agricultural heritage.

At the heart of Graham Street Market lies its wet market section, where an assortment of fresh meats, seafood, and poultry are displayed with precision and care. Here, you'll find butchers skillfully preparing cuts of meat, fishmongers showcasing the day's catch, and vendors offering a variety of live seafood. The wet market provides a glimpse into the city's culinary traditions and showcases the meticulous craftsmanship that has been passed down through generations.

One of the market's most cherished aspects is its role as a community hub. As you engage with the vendors, you're welcomed into a world where personal connections and interactions thrive. The vendors' warm smiles and friendly banter create an environment that fosters a sense of familiarity and belonging. Graham Street Market isn't just a place to shop—it's a place to connect, to share stories, and to build relationships that transcend transactional exchanges.

Beyond the vibrant market scene, Graham Street Market is a testament to Hong Kong's ability to seamlessly blend tradition and modernity. The market's presence in the heart of the bustling Central district is a reminder that amid the skyscrapers and bustling streets, the city's heritage and cultural roots remain intact. The market stands as a bridge between the past and the present, showcasing that even in the midst of rapid urban development, the essence of Hong Kong's culinary traditions endures.

Graham Street Market is more than just a place to buy groceries—it's an immersive experience that engages the senses, stirs curiosity, and celebrates the spirit of Hong Kong. As you navigate the market's vibrant alleys, inhale the intoxicating scents of fresh produce, and engage in conversations with vendors, you become part of a narrative that spans generations and cultures. The market is a celebration of the city's culinary heritage, a testament to its resilience, and an invitation to savor the flavors and stories that shape Hong Kong's culinary identity.

Yum Cha: Where Culinary Art Meets Time-Honored Tradition

In the vibrant culinary landscape of Hong Kong, Yum Cha stands as a beacon of creativity, innovation, and tradition. This iconic dining establishment has transformed the concept of dim sum, elevating it from a mere meal to a captivating culinary art form that fuses tradition with modern flair. With its whimsical presentations, exquisite flavors, and commitment to quality, Yum Cha has become a destination where diners can embark on a sensory journey that transcends taste and engages the imagination.

As you step into Yum Cha, you're immediately enveloped in an ambiance that exudes both elegance and playfulness. The restaurant's décor seamlessly blends classic Chinese motifs with contemporary design elements, setting the stage for the culinary experience that awaits. The tables are adorned with intricate tea sets, charming dumpling baskets, and vibrant tableware, creating an atmosphere that pays homage to tradition while inviting diners to embrace a sense of wonder.

The heart and soul of Yum Cha's offerings lie in its innovative take on dim sum. The restaurant has artfully reimagined classic dim sum dishes, transforming them into edible masterpieces tha delight both the palate and the eye. Each dish is a labor of love, meticulously crafted by skilled chefs who are passionate about pushing the boundaries of culinary creativity. From intricately designed dumplings to playful steamed buns shaped like adorable animals and objects, Yum Cha takes dim sum to new heights.

One of the defining features of Yum Cha is its commitment to blending traditional flavors with modern influences. While the restaurant embraces innovation, it remains deeply rooted in the authenticity of dim sum culture. The iconic Har Gow (shrimp dumplings) and Siew Mai (pork dumplings) are presented with a twist—colorful and creative wrappers that entice diners to explore not only the taste but also the visual delight that each dish offers.

The culinary journey at Yum Cha begins with the visually stunning and irresistibly delectable offerings that arrive at your table. The Charcoal Custard Bun, a signature creation, showcases a jet-black exterior that reveals a luscious and golden custard filling—a harmonious blend of textures and flavors that exemplify the artistry of the restaurant's chefs. The BBQ Piggy Buns are not only adorable but also a testament to Yum Cha's ability to seamlessly merge playfulnes with culinary excellence.

Yum Cha's commitment to presentation is rivaled only by its dedication to flavor. The restaurant's commitment to using the finest ingredients and traditional techniques ensures tha every dish is a symphony of taste that captivates the senses. The delicate balance of sweet, savory, and umami notes in each bite reflects the culinary prowess that Yum Cha brings to its creations.

A visit to Yum Cha is not just about indulging in exquisite cuisine; it's also an immersive experience that encourages diners to engage with their meal on multiple levels. The interactive aspect of dining at Yum Cha is perhaps best embodied by its Tea Time Experience. Servers expertly pour fragrant teas from impressive heights, allowing the tea to aerate and infuse with rich flavors. This tradition pays homage to the essence of yum cha, which translates to "drink tea" in Cantonese—a practice that dates back to ancient China and remains integral to dim sum culture.

The essence of Yum Cha extends beyond its culinary offerings; it's a celebration of shared experiences and the joy of discovery. Diners gather around tables, sharing stories and marveling at the artistic creations before them. The restaurant fosters a sense of togetherness, inviting patrons to immerse themselves in a world of flavors, textures, and conversations.

In conclusion, Yum Cha is a culinary oasis where tradition meets innovation, and where artistry and flavor coalesce to create an unforgettable dining experience. Through its masterful creations, the restaurant invites diners to reimagine the possibilities of dim sum while honoring the heritage that defines it. Yum Cha is not just a restaurant—it's a celebration of culinary craftsmanship, a testament to the beauty of presentation, and a reminder that every meal can be an exploration of taste, culture, and imagination. As you savor each bite and share in the communal joy of dining, you're reminded that Yum Cha is not just a place to eat—it's a culinary journey that leaves an indelible mark on the heart and palate.

Mak's Noodle: A Timeless Culinary Legacy of Flavor and Craftsmanship

Nestled within the bustling streets of Hong Kong, Mak's Noodle stands as a culinary icon that has captured the hearts and palates of locals and visitors alike for generations. With a history spanning over a century, this unassuming eatery has become synonymous with the art of crafting delectable wonton noodles—an art that embodies the essence of Hong Kong's culinary heritage, innovation, and commitment to excellence.

Walking into Mak's Noodle, you're transported into a world where time seems to stand still. The restaurant's humble interiors and traditional décor evoke a sense of nostalgia, harkening back to an era when simplicity and authenticity were prized culinary virtues. Amid the hustle and bustle of modern life, Mak's Noodle offers a respite—a place where the focus is squarely on the timeless craft of creating the perfect bowl of wonton noodles.

At the heart of Mak's Noodle's acclaim lies its signature dish: the wonton noodle soup. While it may seem deceptively simple, the art of crafting this dish is a testament to the culinary expertise that has been passed down through generations. The star of the show is the wonton, delicate parcels of seasoned meat wrapped in translucent skins. Mak's Noodle takes pride in the balance of flavors—the tender wontons, the firm and springy noodles, and the savory broth that ties everything together in a harmonious symphony of taste.

The culinary journey at Mak's Noodle begins with a focus on quality Ingredients. From the fresh succulent shrimp that grace the wontons to the perfectly cooked egg noodles, every element of the dish is carefully selected to ensure an exceptional dining experience. The restaurant's dedication to sourcing the finest ingredients is a reflection of its commitment to upholding the standards that have made it a culinary institution.

One of the hallmarks of Mak's Noodle is its adherence to tradition. The noodle-making process itself is a testament to the craftsmanship that defines the restaurant's reputation. The noodles are hand-pulled, skillfully kneaded and stretched to achieve the ideal texture and thickness. The result is a noodle that is tender yet firm, able to absorb the flavors of the broth without losing its characteristic bite.

The broth, the heart of any noodle soup, is where Mak's Noodle truly shines. The recipe for the broth is a closely guarded secret, passed down through generations and perfected over time. It's a delicate balance of flavors, combining the umami richness of slow-cooked meats with the clarity of a well-crafted stock. The result is a broth that is both comforting and nuanced, a testament to the meticulous approach that defines every aspect of the restaurant's culinary offerings.

Beyond the wonton noodle soup, Mak's Noodle offers an array of dishes that pay homage to Hong Kong's culinary traditions. From crispy spring rolls to beef brisket noodles, each dish reflects the same commitment to quality, flavor, and authenticity that has made the restaurant a household name. Every bite is a journey through the culinary heritage of Hong Kong, a reminder of the flavors that have defined the city's food scene for generations.

The enduring popularity of Mak's Noodle is a testament to its ability to transcend time and trends. In a world where culinary landscapes are constantly evolving, the restaurant remains a constant—a place where diners can savor a taste of history, culture, and tradition. With each bowl of wonton noodle soup, diners are not just experiencing a meal; they are partaking in a culinary legacy that spans over a century and encompasses the essence of Hong Kong's soul.

In conclusion, Mak's Noodle is more than just a restaurant—it's a culinary pilgrimage that honors the past while embracing the present. The restaurant's dedication to quality, tradition, and flavor is evident in every aspect of its offerings. From the hand-pulled noodles to the carefully crafted broth, every element of the dining experience at Mak's Noodle speaks to a commitment to excellence that has stood the test of time. As you savor each bite and appreciate the artistry that goes into each dish, you're reminded that Mak's Noodle is not just a place to eat—it's a celebration of Hong Kong's culinary heritage, a journey through flavors, and a testament to the enduring power of great food to bring people together.

Hong Kong Egg Waffles (Gai Dan Jai): A Delightful Fusion of Tradition and Innovation

In the bustling streets of Hong Kong, the intoxicating aroma of freshly baked delicacies wafts through the air, drawing locals and visitors alike to the source of its origin—the iconic Hong Kong Egg Waffles, locally known as Gai Dan Jai. These delectable treats are more than just a snack; they are a culinary symbol that encapsulates the city's unique blend of tradition, innovation, and street food culture.

The origin of Hong Kong Egg Waffles can be traced back to the 1950s, a time when street vendors sought inventive ways to utilize leftover egg batter. The result was a sweet and crispy waffle that bore a striking resemblance to an egg carton, giving rise to its charming moniker. Over the years, Gai Dan Jai has evolved from a humble street food into a cultural phenomenon, captivating the taste buds of generations and becoming an integral part of Hong Kong's culinary identity.

What sets Hong Kong Egg Waffles apart is their distinctive texture—a harmonious marriage of crispy and chewy that offers a delightful contrast in every bite. The batter is poured into a special mold with spherical cavities, and as it cooks, the heat transforms it into a lattice-like structure that's crispy on the outside and soft on the inside. The end result is a waffle that boasts a delicate balance of flavors and textures, making it a true sensory delight.

While the traditional Gai Dan Jai recipe remains beloved, innovation has led to a plethora of variations that cater to a diverse range of tastes. From matcha-flavored waffles to chocolate-infused creations and even savory renditions featuring cheese and ham, the possibilities are as limitless as the imagination of the chefs and vendors who continue to push the boundaries of this beloved snack. These modern twists on the classic are a testament to Hong Kong's ability to embrace change while honoring tradition.

Gai Dan Jai stands not only as a treat for the palate but also as a visual spectacle that captivates the eye. Vendors skillfully pour the batter into the waffle molds, creating a tantalizing symphony of sizzling sounds and enticing aromas. The resulting waffles are presented in generous portions, their golden hues and intricate patterns beckoning to be savored. Whether enjoyed on the go or while strolling through the bustling streets, Hong Kong Egg Waffles offer a multisensory experience that engages all the senses.

A trip to Hong Kong would be Incom"lete'without a rendezvous with Gai Dan Jai. As you wander through the city's vibrant neighborhoods, you're likely to encounter stalls and kiosks selling these delectable treats, each with its own unique twist on the classic recipe. From traditional street vendors to modern cafes that put a contemporary spin on the waffle, the accessibility of Gai Dan Jai reflects its enduring popularity and its place as a cherished component of Hong Kong's street food culture.

Beyond its immediate culinary appeal, Gai Dan Jai is also a symbol of cultural continuity and resilience. The fact that this simple street food has stood the test of time is a testament to the enduring power of traditions in a rapidly changing world. Each bite of a Hong Kong Egg Waffle carries with it a taste of history and heritage, a connection to the generations of individuals who have enjoyed this treat before us.

In conclusion, Hong Kong Egg Waffles—Gai Dan Jai—are more than just a snack; they are a living embodiment of Hong Kong's cultural fusion, culinary innovation, and street food vibrancy. With their crispy exteriors, chewy interiors, and a myriad of creative interpretations, Gai Dan Jai capture the essence of a city that embraces tradition while embracing the future. As you savor the unique flavors and textures of these delectable waffles, you're reminded that each bite is a journey through time and culture, a celebration of the simple pleasures that bring people together in the heart of Hong Kong's bustling streets.

Mui Kee Congee: A Heartwarming Culinary Tradition

In the heart of bustling Hong Kong, amid the maze of streets and towering skyscrapers, lies a hidden gem that transcends time and culinary trends. Mui Kee Congee, a humble eatery with a storied history, has been serving up bowls of warm comfort and nostalgia for generations. With its roots deeply embedded in traditional Cantonese cuisine, Mui Kee Congee is a haven for those seeking a taste of Hong Kong's culinary heritage and a heartwarming journey through flavors that evoke memories of home.

The story of Mui Kee Congee dates back over six decades, when founder Mak Mui opened a small stall selling congee—a rice porridge known for its simplicity and ability to soothe the soul. From its humble beginnings, Mui Kee Congee has grown into a culinary institution, beloved by locals and food enthusiasts from around the world. Despite its success, the eatery has managed to retain its authenticity and commitment to offering congee that is true to its origins.

The heart of Mui Kee Congee lies In its dedication to crafting congee that reflects the essence of Cantonese cuisine. The congee, a bowl of rice that has been slowly simmered to a creamy consistency, serves as a canvas for an array of toppings and ingredients. From tender slices of pork and velvety century eggs to succulent seafood and fragrant herbs, Mui Kee Congee offers a symphony of flavors that harmonize to create a satisfying and nourishing meal.

One of the most remarkable aspects of Mui Kee Congee is the meticulous attention to detail that goes into every bowl. The congee is cooked with precision, using traditional techniques that have been passed down through generations. The slow simmering process allows the rice grains to release their starch, resulting in a rich and creamy texture that is the hallmark of well-made congee. This attention to detail is a testament to the culinary craftsmanship that has defined the eatery for decades.

Mui Kee Congee's menu is a testament to its commitment to preserving the classics while embracing innovation. While the traditional Pork and Century Egg Congee remains a beloved favorite, the eatery also offers a range of contemporary interpretations that cater to modern tastes. Diners can explore variations such as the Fish Belly and Peanuts Congee or the Abalone and Chicken Congee, each offering a unique combination of flavors and textures.

Beyond the congee itself, Mui Kee is also known for its delectable side dishes that complement the main attraction. From crispy youtiao (Chinese doughnuts) to silky tofu pudding, these accompaniments enhance the dining experience, allowing diners to create their own personalized combinations of flavors and textures. Each side dish is crafted with the same dedication to quality and authenticity that defines Mui Kee Congee.

The ambiance at Mui Kee Congee Is reminiscent of a bygone era—a time when simplicity was celebrated and the focus was on the art of cooking. The eatery's unassuming interiors provide a comforting backdrop to the culinary experience, inviting diners to savor their meals without distraction. It's a space where the aroma of congee fills the air, and the sounds of bustling pots and pans provide a symphony that echoes the rhythm of the kitchen.

A visit to Mui Kee Congee is more than just a meal; it's a journey through time, flavors, and memories. Each spoonful of congee is a reminder of the traditions that have shaped Hong Kong's culinary landscape, a testament to the power of simple ingredients to create culinary magic. Whether enjoyed as a hearty breakfast or a comforting dinner, Mui Kee Congee's offerings transcend cultural boundaries, offering a universal experience of warmth and nourishment.

In conclusion, Mui Kee Congee is a treasure trove of tradition, flavor, and culinary passion that beckons to all who seek the simple pleasures of a well-made bowl of congee. With its time-tested techniques, carefully selected ingredients, and commitment to preserving the essence of Cantonese cuisine, Mui Kee Congee invites diners to embark on a journey through tastes and textures that resonate with the heart and soul. As you savor each spoonful and embrace the comforting warmth of the congee, you're reminded that amidst the fast-paced modernity of Hong Kong, the flavors of the past continue to thrive, offering a taste of home and a celebration of culinary heritage.

Wan Chai Market: A Culinary and Cultural Tapestry of Hong Kong

Nestled within the vibrant neighborhood of Wan Chai in Hong Kong, Wan Chai Market is a dynamic hub that weaves together the threads of history, tradition, and culinary diversity. This bustling market is not just a place to shop for fresh produce and ingredients—it's a microcosm of Hong Kong's rich cultural tapestry, offering a sensory journey through flavors, aromas, and the vibrant spirit of the city.

Wan Chai Market is a multifaceted destination that captures the essence of Hong Kong's bustling street scene. From the moment you step into its energetic atmosphere, you're greeted by a symphony of sounds, colors, and aromas that envelop you in a sensory embrace. The market's alleys are alive with the calls of vendors, the clatter of utensils, and the chatter of shoppers, creating an ambiance that is both invigorating and captivating.

At the heart of Wan Chai Market lies its vibrant wet market, a place where locals and chefs alike converge to source the freshest and finest ingredients. The market is a treasure trove of colors, with stalls overflowing with vibrant fruits, vegetables, seafood, meats, and spices. Each vendor takes pride in displaying their goods with precision and care, creating a visual spectacle that showcases the variety and vitality of Hong Kong's culinary offerings.

One of the most striking aspects of Wan Chai Market is its ability to encapsulate the city's cultural diversity through its culinary offerings. The market is a melting pot of flavors from around the world, reflecting Hong Kong's role as an international hub. You'll find stalls selling traditional Cantonese ingredients side by side with those offering Indian spices, Southeast Asian herbs, and imported European cheeses. This eclectic blend of offerings speaks to the city's open-mindedness and its ability to embrace and celebrate different culinary traditions.

The market is a haven for food enthusiasts seeking authenticity and quality. Wan Chai Market takes pride in its commitment to providing fresh, locally sourced ingredients that adhere to the highest standards. From the succulent seafood caught from the surrounding waters to the aromatic herbs and spices that infuse dishes with flavor, the market's offerings reflect a dedication to culinary excellence that resonates with both home cooks and professional chefs.

Beyond its role as a culinary marketplace, Wan Chai Market also serves as a cultural exchange center—a place where locals and visitors can engage in conversations, share stories, and learn about the various cultures that converge within its bustling aisles. The vendors, with their warm smiles and friendly banter, create an environment that fosters connections and camaraderie. In this sense, Wan Chai Market is not just a place to buy ingredients; it's a space where people from all walks of life come together, united by their love of food and community.

As day transitions into night, Wan Chai Market undergoes a transformation, with its evening market taking center stage. The night market is a sensory feast that offers an array of street food, local snacks, and delicacies that cater to the nocturnal cravings of Hong Kong's residents and visitors. From skewers of grilled meat and seafood to piping hot bowls of noodles and dumplings, the night market is a haven for those seeking a taste of authentic Hong Kong street food culture.

Wan Chai Market's historical significance adds an extra layer of depth to its appeal. The market has been a fixture of the neighborhood for decades, serving as a witness to the evolution of Hong Kong's culinary landscape. Amid the modern skyscrapers that now define Wan Chai, the market stands as a reminder of the city's enduring heritage and its ability to blend the old and the new.

In conclusion, Wan Chai Market is a microcosm of Hong Kong's rich culinary and cultural diversity. Through its bustling wet market, eclectic culinary offerings, and vibrant atmosphere, the market offers a glimpse into the heart and soul of the city. It's a place where tradition and modernity coexist, where flavors from around the world converge, and where connections are formed over shared love for food and community. As you navigate its aisles, inhale the fragrant aromas, and engage with the vendors, you become part of a narrative that celebrates Hong Kong's spirit, resilience, and the joy of exploring its culinary treasures.

CONCLUSION:

Language and Communication: Unveiling the Tapestry of Hong Kong's Diversity

In the vibrant tapestry of Hong Kong's cultural landscape, language and communication play a pivotal role in shaping the city's identity, fostering connections, and reflecting its unique blend of traditions and influences. As a dynamic metropolis that serves as a global crossroads, Hong Kong is a melting pot of languages, dialects, and communication styles, each contributing to the rich mosaic that defines the city's vibrant social fabric.

At the heart of Hong Kong's linguistic diversity is its status as a Special Administrative Region of China. As such, the official languages are both Chinese and English, showcasing the city's historical connection to British colonial rule and its integration with the broader Chinese cultural sphere. Cantonese, a prominent Chinese dialect, is the most widely spoken language in Hong Kong and serves as a symbol of local identity and heritage.

Cantonese, known as "Yueyu" in Mandarin, is more than just a language—it's a window into the heart and soul of Hong Kong's culture. Its distinctive tonal qualities, rich vocabulary, and colloquial expressions reflect the city's dynamic spirit and its blend of traditional values with modern aspirations. Cantonese is not only spoken in daily interactions but also encapsulates the essence of Hong Kong's music, film, and literature, allowing its cultural nuances to flourish.

While Cantonese is the mother tongue of many Hong Kong residents, the city's linguistic landscape is a reflection of its international character. English, as the other official language, plays a significant role in Hong Kong's administrative, educational, and business sectors. Its presence is a testament to Hong Kong's history as a British colony and its global connectivity, making it an essential tool for cross-cultural communication and trade.

Beyond Cantonese and English, the multicultural nature of Hong Kong is evident in the diverse range of languages and dialects spoken within its communities. Mandarin Chinese, with its increasing prominence on the global stage, is becoming more prevalent due to its status as the national language of China. Additionally, a multitude of languages from around the world can be heard throughout the city, reflecting the presence of expatriates, immigrants, and tourists.

he fusion of languages in Hong Kong is not just a matter of communication—it's a celebration f diversity and a bridge that connects people from different backgrounds. As you navigate the ity's bustling streets, you'll hear a symphony of languages, from Tagalog and Indonesian to rench and Hindi. This linguistic kaleidoscope mirrors the city's role as a meeting point for ultures and a beacon of multiculturalism.

n daily life, language acts as a conduit for connection, allowing Hong Kong residents to express hemselves, share ideas, and build relationships. It's not only about functional communication ut also about the cultural nuances that words carry. The way greetings are exchanged, the dioms that pepper conversations, and the body language that accompanies speech all ontribute to the intricate dance of interpersonal connections.

he use of language extends beyond spoken words. Hong Kong's rich visual landscape is narked by bilingual signage, showcasing both Chinese and English characters. Street signs, shop ames, and public transportation announcements are all displayed in both languages, creating sense of accessibility for residents and visitors alike. This bilingual environment not only acilitates navigation but also reflects the city's commitment to inclusivity and global ommunication.

n the digital age, language and communication have taken on new dimensions through social nedia platforms, messaging apps, and online communities. Hong Kong's tech-savvy population ngages in conversations, shares news, and participates in discussions that transcend eographical boundaries. Social media has become a platform for expression, activism, and ultural exchange, allowing Hong Kong's residents to connect with the world at large.

anguage also intersects with cultural identity and social dynamics. As Hong Kong evolves, ebates about linguistic preservation and the balance between tradition and progress arise. he ongoing exploration of what it means to be Hong Kongese—the fusion of heritage and lobalization—finds its reflection in language and communication.

n conclusion, language and communication form the threads that weave together the intricate apestry of Hong Kong's cultural landscape. The coexistence of Cantonese, English, and a nultitude of other languages reflects the city's international character and its history as a global rossroads. Through language, residents and visitors alike experience the vibrancy of Hong ong's multicultural fabric, forge connections, and celebrate the nuances that make this netropolis a captivating fusion of tradition and modernity. As you navigate the streets, onverse with locals, and engage in the cultural tapestry, you become part of the narrative that efines Hong Kong's identity—one that embraces diversity, connectivity, and the universal ower of communication.

Conclusion: Unveiling the Dynamic Charm of Hong Kong in 2024

As we draw the curtains on our immersive journey through the Hong Kong Travel Guide for 2024, we find ourselves captivated by the dynamic charm and kaleidoscope of experiences that this enchanting metropolis has to offer. From the dizzying heights of its towering skyscrapers to the serene tranquility of its lush landscapes, Hong Kong beckons travelers with a fusion of tradition and innovation that is unlike any other.

Exploring Hong Kong in 2024 is a voyage that encompasses a rich mosaic of cultural diversity, historical significance, and culinary delights. From the iconic neighborhoods of Central and Sheung Wan to the bustling streets of Tsim Sha Tsui and Kowloon, every corner of this city tells a story—a story of resilience, progress, and a vibrant collision of cultures that has shaped Hong Kong into the multifaceted gem it is today.

The city's world-renowned attractions, such as Victoria Peak and Hong Kong Disneyland, provide glimpses into the spectrum of experiences that Hong Kong offers. Beyond these iconic sites, we've delved into the hidden treasures of Lantau Island, explored the tranquility of Tai O Fishing Village, and traversed the cultural significance of Avenue of Stars and Ocean Park. Each destination contributes to the multifaceted tapestry of experiences that await travelers in Hong Kong.

But it's not just the places that define Hong Kong—it's the people, the culture, and the culinary scene that truly set it apart. We've journeyed through local cuisine markets, sampled exquisite dim sum at Yum Cha, and sipped tea in traditional tea houses, all while uncovering the stories behind each dish and savoring the heritage that flavors bring to life. And let's not forget the diverse range of accommodations, from luxury hotels like The Ritz-Carlton and Four Seasons to boutique gems like Madera Hollywood and iclub Sheung Wan Hotel, ensuring that every traveler finds their perfect home away from home.

Language and communication play a crucial role in the city's identity, fostering connections that transcend geographical boundaries. The linguistic symphony of Cantonese, English, and a myriad of other languages paints a vivid picture of Hong Kong's multicultural fabric and its ability to embrace diversity in all its forms.

At the heart of this guide lies the exploration of Hong Kong's international airports—Hong Kong International Airport (HKG) and Shenzhen Bao'an International Airport (SZX). These gateways not only facilitate seamless travel but also epitomize the city's spirit of innovation, efficiency, and global connectivity. The inception, design, sustainability efforts, and the way they blend air and land travel represent Hong Kong's commitment to progress and hospitality.

Through the lens of travel, we've explored the city's historical background, cultural diversity, and the best times to visit. We've delved into visa and entry requirements, currency matters, health and safety tips, and a comprehensive packing guide to ensure that every traveler embarks on their journey with confidence and preparedness.

Hong Kong, with its ever-evolving landscape and its fusion of tradition and modernity, promises to captivate the hearts and minds of those who venture into its embrace. It's a place where the past dances with the future, where culinary delights tell stories of heritage, and where every corner holds the promise of discovery.

As you prepare to embark on your journey to Hong Kong, armed with insights, tips, and a sense of wonder, remember that this guide is a mere glimpse into the treasures that await. Beyond the words on these pages, the true magic of Hong Kong lies in the experiences that you'll create, the people you'll meet, and the memories you'll carry with you. So, pack your bags, embrace the adventure, and allow Hong Kong to weave its enchanting spell as you explore, connect, and immerse yourself in the vibrant energy of this captivating metropolis in the year 2024.

Made in United States
Troutdale, OR
01/03/2024

16652954R00075